GROWN-UP ABUSED CHILDREN

GROWN-UP ABUSED CHILDREN

By

JAMES LEEHAN, M.A., M.S.S.A.

Associate Director
University Christian Movement
Cleveland, Ohio

and

LAURA PISTONE WILSON, Ph.D.

Associate Dean
Student Group Services
Cleveland State University
Cleveland, Ohio

CHARLES C THOMAS • PUBLISHER
Springfield • Illinois • U.S.A.

Published and Distributed Throughout the World by
CHARLES C THOMAS • PUBLISHER
2600 South First Street
Springfield, Illinois 62717

This book is protected by copyright. No part of it may be reproduced in any manner without written permission from the publisher.

© *1985 by* CHARLES C THOMAS • PUBLISHER
ISBN 0-398-05106-X
Library of Congress Catalog Card Number: 85-2605

With THOMAS BOOKS *careful attention is given to all details of manufacturing and design. It is the Publisher's desire to present books that are satisfactory as to their physical qualities and artistic possibilities and appropriate for their particular use.* THOMAS BOOKS *will be true to those laws of quality that assure a good name and good will.*

Printed in the United States of America
Q-R-3

Library of Congress Cataloging in Publication Data

Leehan, James.
   Grown-up abused children.

   Bibliography: p.
   Includes index.
   1. Adult child abuse victims. 2. Group psychotherapy. I. Wilson, Laura Pistone. II. Title.
RC569.5.C55L44   1985   616.89   85-2605
ISBN 0-398-05116-X

FOREWORD

ALTHOUGH REPORTS of child abuse mushroomed in the late 1970s and early 1980s, nearly everyone involved in the problem agrees that this rise hides an important fact: child abuse is not a new problem. Past generations of children suffered from this problem, probably as much, maybe more so, than the current generation, and much less of the abuse in the past came to public attention or received any kind of professional help.

This raises the question, what responsibility does society have towards these past generations of abused children? The responsibility is two-fold. On the one hand, we know the long-term damage that child abuse can cause, and it is only fair and appropriate that we should organize to assist these victims of another generation. Indeed, if our emerging research is correct, responding to these victims is an important step that we need to take to cope with a whole range of other social problems from crime to suicide to sexual deviance. But at the same time, society has another responsibility. In the rush to draw public attention to the seriousness of the problem on child abuse, we have had a tendency to overstate the inevitability of its traumatic effects. Those who were abused as children also need reassurance that they are not permanently maimed, that many of their efforts to cope and put their past behind them have made them strong and capable individuals.

This book is one of the few which looks seriously at this problem of child abuse victims grown up. It is badly needed. Many such victims are clients of the mental health system and our society's more informal counseling systems, and yet few guidelines exist for work with this population.

The book should be helpful to three groups in particular. The book can and should be read by former victims to realize that they are not alone, that others suffered what they have and are experiencing many of the same effects that they do, that the problems that they have are not unique and not a sign of inevitable disaster.

The book will also be very useful to human service professionals, who will see the connection between many of the presenting problems of their clients and a history of abuse in the past. The book will encourage mental health practitioners to take these problems seriously and will give them ideas for new treatment methods that they can use in ongoing individual and group therapy.

The book may have some special usefulness for professionals involved in college counseling programs, since much of the practice that informs this book occurred in the course of work in a college setting. This book is a welcome addition to the growing effort to respond in a sensitive and humane way to the victims of one of our society's most chronic and poignant disasters.

DAVID FINKELHOR
Family Violence Research Program
University of New Hampshire
Durham, New Hampshire

PREFACE

A FEW years ago a social service professor at Cleveland State University taught a class on child abuse. Following that class several students approached her individually and shared the fact that they were former victims of abuse. For all of them this was the first time they had discussed their abuse experience with anyone. They also felt that they were the only persons to whom this had happened. The sense of isolation and fear they conveyed was profound.

This professor later shared these experiences with a campus minister at the University. He had himself encountered a similar sense of secrecy and shame from individual counsellees who had finally been able to discuss their abusive experience. As the two discussed the issue, it seemed appropriate to invite these various people to meet with one another in order to share their experiences and break down the sense of isolation. The students were approached individually about the prospect and, with a mixture of eagerness and reticence, most of them agreed to give it a try.

Although the first meeting began hesitantly, a great sense of relief soon pervaded the room as one after another the students revealed their past experiences of abuse and their present struggles to overcome the fear and distrust that seemed to rule their lives. This group continued to meet weekly for six months until graduations, jobs, and summer schedules forced them to discontinue. In those few months, the members gained new friends, new insights into what had happened to them, new skills for developing and maintaining interpersonal relationships, and a profound relief from the guilt and isolation that had plagued them for years. They no longer perceived themselves as bad children who deserved the treatment they had received.

In the years since that first group for grown-up abused children was convened, several others have been conducted. The groups have lasted from six months to over a year. The almost universal reaction of participants is that of relief and release as they are finally freed to discuss the deep, dark secret of their abusive past.

For the first four years publicity for the groups was restricted to campus publications aimed specifically at students. Frequently, however, the group leaders were contacted by people off campus who had heard about the group and were interested in participating. Whenever possible, they were accommodated. Unfortunately, schedules did not always coincide and groups were often filled.

It soon became clear that this type of service was also needed in the community. Finally, group leaders agreed to more extensive publicity (an article in a city newspaper and some university public service programs on public radio). In just a few weeks they were inundated with more than 40 requests to participate. With the help of a grant from the Episcopal Diocese of Ohio, additional group leaders were trained and new groups started. However, the demand continues to exceed the available leadership. Although no further publicity has been done, new requests are still received from those wanting to participate. By the spring of 1984 six different groups were meeting throughout the Greater Cleveland community under the joint sponsorship of Parents Anonymous of Northeastern Ohio and the University Christian Movement.

So the casual campus conversation which led to the formation of the first grown-up abused children group has also resulted in a whole network of support groups throughout the city. However, for those of us who have become involved in the program that conversation has opened up a new appreciation of the complexity of child abuse. We have come to a new understanding of the wide range of effects that experience can have on the lives of those who have been subjected to it.

We were all aware of child abuse as a problem in our society. It has received increasing attention in the last few years as more and more incidents are being reported by physicians, social workers, teachers, and school counselors. The media is reporting incidents and examining causes. Programs are being developed to protect the child victims and to provide treatment for the abusive parents, many of whom were abused themselves.

Legislation has been enacted making it mandatory to report suspected incidents of child abuse. Child abuse hot lines have been established, and organizations like Parents Anonymous have developed special programs to deal with the needs of abusive parents and teach them new parenting skills. Most mental health treatment centers now offer family counseling, and researchers have begun to study family dynamics and personality variables that seem related to spouse and child abuse.

However, even with this flurry of attention, one part of the population related to the abuse problem has not received much attention — grown-up abused children, the adult survivors of child abuse. Each year thousands of children in our society experience abuse in a variety of forms — physical, sexual, verbal, and emotional. And each year thousands of these same children grow into adulthood and strive to develop meaningful relationships and satisfying adult lives. Unfortunately these former victims of abuse carry with them many secret pains and frustrations, many unresolved fears and a multitude of emotional wounds which have never healed and which seriously hinder their ability to function as mature, productive adults.

Unless or until a former abuse victim is identified as an abusive parent, the community offers no treatment program for the former victim. The community seems to assume that when a person moves into adulthood the effects of the abusive background will disappear. The problem is over and the child will "grow out of" any difficulties or psychological disabilities caused by physical or sexual abuse or neglect. Few, if any, community programs are available to assist former victims in overcoming the effects that the abuse may have had on their developmental process. And this dearth of treatment opportunities continues despite the growing understanding in the human service profession regarding the process of psychological development.

It is the belief of the authors and of the many people who have worked with grown-up abused children groups in the past few years, that much more needs to be done to develop understanding of and treatment modalities for the long-term effects of child abuse. The deficiencies which these people have experienced in their developmental process are not going to be compensated for unless and until they are recognized, taken seriously, and corrected.

The fact that most abuse victims were deprived of many developmental opportunities and that they received clearly conflicting, contradictory and even false messages about themselves must be accounted for in any kind of treatment. The impact of these experiences does not simply disappear or automatically diminish when one reaches adulthood.

A central goal of this book, then, is to describe the major, recurring problems faced by these adults which hinder or preclude their ability to function in a happy, healthy, and productive manner. While these problems are not unique in and of themselves, for these adults the cumulative effect of their negative childhood experiences makes the issues more intense. If we view these problems as an interrelated and self-perpetuating cluster, and place them in a developmental framework with a history of abuse and neglect, the need for a treatment of the whole becomes clear. As one of these adults once stated, "When I stopped trying to deal with each issue one at a time and realized that they were all linked together and tied to my abusive past, it became easier to understand what I was up against and what I needed."

For many of these adults what seems most effective is a special form of group counseling. A second focus of this book, then, is to describe a successful group treatment strategy and discuss why and how it works. This intervention has proven effective when used by itself and in conjunction with individual therapy. The specific goals for these groups will be described. Unique characteristics of the groups will be highlighted, including how they differ from other forms of group psychotherapy. In particular, the role of group leaders and special problems of transference and counter-transference will be explored. Case studies and examples are interspersed throughout the text to show the relationship between the abuse experience, the problems of adulthood and the therapeutic value of these support groups.

The authors hope that these materials will assist professionals in developing forms of treatment for the many child abuse victims in our society who have had the good fortune to survive into adulthood. We hope that the adult years of these former victims can be less painful than their childhood and that they can become contented and productive members of our society.

Many people and organizations have helped to make this book possible. The first person who must be thanked is Professor Elizabeth Carmichael Smith whose sensitive presentation of the problem of child abuse in her Social Service class enabled her students to discuss their own experiences with her. Her responsiveness to their needs really motivated the formation of the first group. Dr. Christine Courtois worked with the second group while she was at the Counseling Center at Cleveland State University and her insights were crucial in the formulation of the initial analysis of individual needs and group process concerns. We are especially grateful to the Christian Church in Ohio for the Reconciliation Grant it provided to help with the early development of these materials. Also, thanks must be given to the board of managers of the University Christian Movement in Cleveland for their strong support for the entire grown-up abused children program. Additionally, Robert Clarke, the director of the UCM, must be thanked not only for his support and encouragement but for the insight he provided from his own experience of leading a group.

The authors would also like to thank Angie Leehan and John Wilson. First, we owe them a vote of appreciation for their patience, support, and forebearance as they allowed the time and schedule adjustments necessary for us to complete the task. Second, we offer our gratitude for their special forms of assistance: John for his professional insights and suggestions; Angie for making our editing process so much easier with her trusty word processor. We are also grateful to Kathy Soltis for her many expert suggestions in our editing process. Thank you also to our artist friend, Larry Pillot, for his logo design which has been used in publicity for the program and on the cover of this book. Several of the secretaries at Cleveland State University deserve thanks for typing initial drafts: Lauretta Stockmaster, Deborah Kirkpatrick, Rita Rydelis, Mary Erdani, Claudia Coletta, and Mary Elizabeth Wozniak.

Of course, none of this would have been possible were it not for the former abuse victims who have participated in the groups. They overcame the paralyzing guilt and fear which had been instilled in them, revealed their experiences, and shared their struggles. Some even offered suggestions about the contents of this book. Without their courage and strong instinct for survival none of this would have been possible. Thank you all!

JAMES LEEHAN
LAURA WILSON

CONTENTS

	Page
Preface	vii

Chapter One: *The Grown-up Abused Child as an Individual*	3
Recurrent Problems	3
Lack of Trust	4
Low Self-Esteem	6
Lack of Interpersonal Skills	11
Sense of Helplessness	13
Lack of Decision Making Skills	13
Dealing with Feelings	16
Other Problems	20
Sexual Problems	20
Flashbacks and Nightmares	23
Framework for Understanding	24

Chapter Two: *Goals and Strategies for Support Group*	26
Breaking the Sense of Isolation	27
Providing a Supportive Environment	29
Providing Consistency to Promote Trust	32
Providing Opportunities for Problem Solving	38
Learning to Express and Deal with Feelings	40
Learning Interpersonal Skills	47

Chapter Three: *The Grown-up Abused Child in the Group*	52
Advantages of Group Treatment	52
The Reality Factor	52
Safe Environment	55

Arenas for Practice.................................... 56
　Complications in Group Treatment......................... 56
　　Distorted Communication............................... 57
　　Sensitivity as a Defense Mechanism 59
　　The Acceptance of Acceptance 63
　　Comfort with Chaos.................................... 65
　　Goal Setting 66
　　Safety in Similarity.................................. 69
　　Feedback 72
　Conclusion... 74
Chapter Four: *The Group Leader*............................ 75
　Understanding 75
　Patient 80
　Responsive to Feelings................................... 85
　Comfortable with Themselves 91
　Firm 97
　Role Models 100

GROWN-UP
ABUSED
CHILDREN

CHAPTER ONE

THE GROWN-UP ABUSED CHILD AS AN INDIVIDUAL

WHILE it is true that the problems in living experienced by grown-up abused children are similar in many ways to those of other individuals, the manifestations are frequently more intense and more difficult to confront and to alter. We believe that most of these problems can be directly traced to childhood experiences marked by frequent, continued physical or sexual abuse or neglect. After several years of working with support groups for grown-up abused children, we have identified five major recurring problems which often profoundly hinder or prevent the adult from functioning as a happy, healthy, and productive individual.

Many of these symptoms have been noted previously by other professionals (Helfer, 1978). Briefly, these problems include: (1) a basic sense of mistrust toward self and others and a consequent inability to establish deep meaningful interpersonal and sexual relationships; (2) deeply ingrained feelings of low self-worth which are frequently reflected in disparaging self statements and the belief that "no one could possibly care about me because I'm not worth it;" (3) lack of expertise in basic social skills which further impedes the ability to establish friendships and other relationships; (4) a sense of helplessness which frequently results in an inability to make decisions and is manifested in many lives by haphazard, seemingly unplanned life goals and events; and (5) difficulty in identifying, acknowledging, and disclosing feelings, especially evident in the underlying, frequently debilitating, unresolved feelings of anger, guilt, and depression. Of course, not all grown-up abused children exhibit all of these characteristics, but they occur frequently enough in greater or lesser degree to be noteworthy.

We will consider each of these problems as well as their attendant sets of beliefs, attitudes, and behaviors in greater depth. As appropriate, and wherever possible, a theoretical framework of psychosocial development will be provided so that the effects of abuse can be traced back to the origins of these symptoms and followed through later development. By analyzing where "things went wrong," or "what was missing" during the early developmental stages one can understand why certain seemingly irrational or unfounded behaviors and beliefs persist into adulthood and interfere with adult life relationships.

LACK OF TRUST

One virtually universal problem identified by grown-up abused children themselves is the great difficulty they have in learning to trust others and develop close interpersonal relationships. We believe that this inability to trust others is the basis for almost all the other problems these adults face.

Developmentally, establishing trust is one of the first requirements for healthy personality formation. Indeed, in Erikson's (1963) theory of human development, the first psychosocial crisis all humans encounter is the trust vs. mistrust conflict. This stage begins at birth and continues as a major focus until approximately age one and one-half.* During this time the infant/child learns to trust the prime caretaker, usually the mother, and from this experience to trust himself or herself. This sense of trust implies that "one has learned to rely on the sameness and continuity of the outer providers, but also that one may trust oneself . . . and one is trustworthy" (Erikson, 1963, page 248). In order for this trust to develop effectively the mother needs to be nurturing and consistent so the child can learn that certain behaviors will elicit predictable, consistent responses. In the case of abused children the mother frequently is not predictable or consistent in her behavior, reactions, and attitudes toward the child. Behaviors that receive

---

*All age spans are approximations which vary from person to person within a fairly definable range.

laughter and applause on one day, may be met with verbal or physical punishment on another day. Because of this the child does not learn to trust his or her mother, the environment, or others — in fact, he or she learns *not* to trust them.

Since it is often the case that the child cannot distinguish which behaviors result in certain responses, the abused child learns not to trust him or herself. The child's behavior frequently becomes cautious and watchful, a characteristic that often continues on into adulthood. The grown-up abused child may act tentatively, testing carefully for responses from others, providing caveats and qualifications before committing to an opinion or action.

In addition, when these adults finally reach the point of wanting to trust someone, this process is frequently interrupted by the need to "test" the person whom they want so desperately to care for and trust. The testing will take a variety of forms, but the end message is always the same, "Prove that you still love me by tolerating one more unfair demand or passing one more test." Needless to say, this testing is self-defeating and at times results in the loss of a friend or loved one, thus confirming what the adult believed from the beginning — that is, that he or she was not worthy or deserving of being loved.

The following case study will illustrate more graphically some of the problems discussed in this section.

> Marie was a 23-year-old college honor student, outstandingly bright, but equally insecure and afraid to trust or be close to people. She lived with her father and stepmother, an uneasy arrangement since her father, though no longer physically abusive continued to harass and criticize her verbally and emotionally. She had lost her mother during her adolescence through an apparent suicide. By the time she joined the group in her early 20s, she had perfected an intricate, self-protective system of complex defenses that kept her safely distant from, though apparently related to, other people. In daily life, she had several friends who knew little or nothing about her abusive history and who found her to be a witty, charming, and at times brilliant, conversationalist and also a steadfast, loyal friend. Within the group, for the entire first year she barely spoke a word and appeared frightened and withdrawn, though obviously attentive.
>
> Finally, during the second year the female leader was able to break through the isolation and loneliness and began to draw Marie out. The cause of the initial breakthrough remains an enigma. It appears that the female leader and Marie shared some intuitive affinity for one another, perhaps a basic understanding of the intense need that Marie had to be loved and cared for. At any rate, the long, slow process of learning to open

up and trust was begun. Frequently, it was a "one step forward, three steps backward" procedure. One week Marie would feel safe and begin to disclose her past and her needs. The following three meetings she would be unable to utter a word for fear of being hurt or punished for sharing. As the female leader and other group members continued to offer support and reassurance over time, the need for Marie to retreat back into herself diminished.

What happened next showed her increased strength and trust as well as her continuing insecurity and need for reassurance. She began to test the female leader. She would call her at home at times when she knew it would be difficult for the leader to talk with her and provide support. She would make greater demands on the leader's time outside the group, waiting to see if the leader would reject her. Through it all she would also remain self-effacing and passive-aggressive, laying out the demands and waiting in terror for the leader to take the responsibility and provide reassurance one more time.

Interestingly, as the relationship between the two continued to develop, the demands peaked and the testing became more intermittent. A turning point was reached when the leader finally confronted Marie with the impossibility of meeting all her needs. The leader expressed her own frustration at not being able to "do it all" because she was also a fallible, human being. This revelation to Marie seemed to change the nature of the relationship, making it more equal.

For many grown-up abused children, the fear of rejection and the need for support and reassurance are with them to a greater or lesser degree for the remainder of their lives. If they are able to become more aware of these needs and discern when they are testing or making unfair demands on others, they can begin to take greater control over their own behavior. They can learn more direct ways of asking people for what they need and realize that another's inability to always meet their needs is a human failing and not a sign of rejection. This insight can free them and allow them to begin to trust others.

LOW SELF-ESTEEM

A second problem arises out of the inability to learn to trust others and oneself. According to Erikson (1963, page 248), the ability to trust oneself and others "forms a basis in the child for a sense of identity which will later combine a sense of being 'all right,' of being oneself, and of becoming what other people trust one will become." We have found that the abused child typically does not believe that he or she is "all right." In fact, the contrary message is internalized. When one is repeatedly told that one is not all right, that one is stupid or ugly or unloveable, and incapable of doing things, one begins to believe it. Children internalize those statements and feel ashamed and unworthy, not good enough to be cared about or valued. The child believes that there is something inherently wrong with him or her for why else would one's mother continually reject, punish, and verbally confirm one's lack of worth? In brief, "if your own mother doesn't like you, who will?" And the conclusion which follows is "therefore, there must be something wrong with me." In our groups we have found that even as adults, these individuals often express feelings of not being "all right," of being unworthy of friends or caring behaviors from others.

In part, this belief stems from what the adult learned as a child from the abusive parent. The abusive parent frequently does not differentiate between the child as a person and the child's behavior. Thus, unacceptable behavior is not identified. Rather, the parent tells the child (and the child comes to believe) that he or she is bad because of what he or she does. More often than not, the expectations that abusive parents have for their children are unrealistic or impossible. For example, in many instances abusive parents act like children themselves and expect their children to take care of them. This type of role reversal is obviously unfair and even the brightest, most able children are unable to meet the demands that are placed upon them. Thus, they meet with parental criticism, derision as well as physical abuse. These children do not realize that what is expected is really too much and instead they internalize the feelings of incompetence, unworthiness and "badness." Clearly, in reality, the problem lies in the parents' inability to affirm the child as a worthwhile human being, and to differentiate between the child as a person and the child's behavior.

Coupled with this is a fear associated with believing that others might sincerely like or care about the person, a phenomenon that one group member has called "waiting for the other shoe to drop." This fear manifests itself in the belief that, "If people say they like me or are kind to me, I know that sooner or later something bad will happen; they will hurt me in some way." That occurrence of something "bad" has been the only consistency in their lives. Sometimes the pressure of waiting for the "bad" to come is so great that the grown-up abused child will actually behave in some self-defeating way or manipulate the situation to bring about a negative consequence, just to relieve the tension.

For example,

At one group meeting, we reviewed the progress members were making toward achieving their goals. One of Jeff's goals was to overcome his extreme shyness and talk more, both at the group meeting and in other settings. He had made substantial progress on this goal in the group setting. He no longer needed to be cajoled, prodded, or pleaded with before voicing an opinion. Members were very positive and enthusiastic about the gains he had made. One could see by the expression on his face that he truly enjoyed all the attention and praise he was receiving. He seemed to glow with happiness.

At the next few meetings his behavior began to change. He was tense and irritable and became more and more silent. He finally regressed to a point where his behavior was similar to what it had been when he first joined the group. Members and group leaders alike were mystified, as well as frustrated, by the change.

After much discussion, it finally became clear that Jeff, at least unconsciously, was deliberately reverting back to his old way of behaving. After receiving all the positive reinforcement at the meeting weeks before, he had become nervous and afraid, waiting for the rejection, pain, and hurt that always followed whenever he felt good about something.

Fortunately, members could understand and empathize with his feelings and offered support and reassurance. In time his behavior changed again, this time in a positive direction and he regained his self-confidence.

This example illustrates several of the points discussed above: the fears and beliefs grown-up abused children have acquired about "bad" always following "good"; the feelings of not being truly loveable; the belief that they are not "all right" and do not deserve love and caring from others. Hopefully by having the experience where "good" follows "good" on a consistent basis, they can begin to overcome these fears and beliefs and will not have to "make bad things" happen each time they have a positive experience.

The tendency towards self-defeating behavior also occurs in other areas of the adult's life, such as failure to complete courses of study, a chronic "dropping in and out" of college classes, lack of follow-through in job searching or on work-related projects. It has been our experience in at least four groups of grown-up abused children composed almost entirely of college students, that anxiety levels and fear of failure related to college coursework often become debilitating. Even in the case of extremely bright students who have records of high achievement, the fear of failure and the high anxiety sometimes win out and the student either drops the course or does poorly on tests and assignments even when well prepared. This almost seems to be an unconscious confirmation of one's inferiority and inability to do well and becomes a self-fulfilling prophecy. Even repeated successes do not erase the learned belief in one's inadequacy.

Another consequence of these feelings of inadequacy is the inability to ask for anything for oneself. This generally comes from the belief that one is not worthy of receiving love, attention, rewards, or anything positive. This belief is compounded by the fact that when something positive happens (for example, when a "reward" is earned and received or attention is given) the initial reaction is of guilt ("I don't deserve this") followed by a devaluing or discounting of one's own actions.

Further, we have observed repeatedly that these adults have great difficulty taking any credit for achievements or for having caused something good to happen. Again, this reaction seems to stem directly from childhood experiences in which they were punished or "put down" when they succeeded. Often, they were accused of being selfish or prideful or arrogant when they merely expressed joy or satisfaction at an achievement.

As adults, they are so uncertain that they can have an effect on the world that when they do, they attribute the result to external circumtances or other people or they belittle their own efforts. They make comments like, "I was lucky" or "It was really easy." One group member went so far as to attribute his success on a test to the fact that it had snowed that day. Obviously, there was no logical connection between his achievement and the weather, but he simply could not take credit for himself or his ability.

Further, these adults have a difficult time listening to and believing praise for their own actions or abilities which comes from others. Perhaps this is because they never received very much praise or other positive reinforcement for their efforts. Interestingly, they feel free to give praise to others but are noticeably uncomfortable when they are praised.

Still another, quite different, reaction is a kind of narcissistic overcompensation, or self-aggrandisement. These adults may make grandiose statements about their talents or intelligence. Even though these statements are objectively accurate, the talents and intelligence of these adults have not resulted in productive achievements. In fact, many of these adults are quite bright and talented, and they are angry and bitter that their lives have not been such that their gifts were nurtured and developed. While this anger is often quite understandable, it becomes dysfunctional when used as an excuse for continued lack of action, productivity, or goal-setting. Further, these boastful statements often alienate or intimidate others, resulting in increased feelings of isolation and loneliness.

Several examples of this low self-esteem coupled with self-defeating behavior readily comes to mind.

> One is the case of Jerry, a thirty-six-year-old man, who has been employed only occasionally. He still lives with his parents who continue to be disparaging of his abilities and neglectful of his needs. Though exceptionally intelligent, especially in mathematics, repeated attempts at college all ended in only partial success or failure. Jerry alternates between considering himself a failure and striking out at a world that is insensitive to his needs and his gifts. He vehemently asserts to all who will listen how high his I.Q. is and how colleges are not designed to meet the needs of geniuses. He feels the need for a one-on-one nurturing of his abilities and talents, not the traditional classroom approach of one teacher to twenty or thirty students. Thus, he blames his lack of success on his unwillingness to bend to a system that he considers inhuman.
>
> Jerry received much support as well as hard feedback from group members and particularly the male group leader about the self-defeating nature of his behavior. He was encouraged to try things that had a reasonable hope of success and received support, reassurance and consolation even when the attempts were not successful. Over time he was able to become assertive in a more positive way instead of criticizing the "system" that he perceived as holding him back.

That there is some fact in Jerry's belief is true; however, there is also the part of him that fears that were he to actually find someone who provided a one-on-one experience, he just might not succeed. Thus, his attempts at reaching out become carefully structured to elicit rejection.

We have attempted to illustrate the three patterns of self-defeating behavior that we have observed grown-up abused children use in an effort to protect themselves from hurt or disappointment. Each of the patterns stem from the low self-esteem experienced by these adults. The underlying beliefs, fears, and feelings of inadequacy are deeply ingrained and the behavioral responses are often unconscious. Even in cases where the adult is aware of the behavior, change is difficult to enact.

The intentional "messing up" offers a relief from the tension that builds as these adults wait for something bad to happen. They believe that bad things will happen to them because they do not deserve anything good. For the same reason, they cannot ask for anything for themselves or take credit for their accomplishments, except in the extreme case where they take too much credit and become grandiose.

In the next chapter we will discuss how we used the group process to change these false beliefs and allay the fears so that these adults can come to like themselves, feel positive about their achievements, and begin to feel entitled to a good life.

INABILITY TO MAKE FRIENDS

The lack of trust and the feelings of low self-worth which characterize grown-up abused children seem to come together most painfully when the individual goes out into the world and attempts to establish relationships with other people. When the child grows old enough to attend school, teachers and peers become increasingly important. As the child starts to interact with other children and adults he or she learns that the interactions with the parents in the home are not necessarily typical or appropriate. In one way, this is a useful insight which causes the child to learn more positive social behaviors and skills; however, it also dramatizes the abnormality of the home environment and the child's lack of appropriate behaviors. Feelings of inadequacy rapidly become feelings of inferiority; comparisons of self to others always end up with the self being not as good, or even worthless. Recognition of the abnormality of the home situation can result in greater shame and extreme introversion as the child tries to keep others from finding out about the abuse. This secretiveness, coupled with the feelings of low self-esteem, lack of interactive skills, and inability to trust others, greatly limits the child's ability to develop friendships and effectively resolve the pressing psychosocial crises which revolve around doing things beside and with others (Erikson, 1963).

We have observed that the lack of social skills continues into adolescence and adulthood so that many grown-up abused children find themselves unable to share personal information or to acknowledge or disclose their feelings. They are therefore unable to develop deep, meaningful relationships with others.

Most of these adults have never had the experience of conversations with parents and have limited their own interactions with other children. They have never learned, or had the opportunity to practice, these communication skills and behaviors with others and feel inadequate and embarrassed that as adults they still cannot do what seems to come so naturally to others. They often feel that people don't pay attention to them. Even when they try to initiate conversation, they don't receive the type of response they want. They believe it is because they don't know the correct words or behaviors and end up feeling awkward and clumsy.

Even when the adult has been able to learn enough social skills to project a fairly extroverted exterior, the inability to trust is just beneath the surface, and the net result is a number of superficial, friendly relationships which lack depth and are not satisfying or sufficient. They often have strong needs for intimacy which have grown out of the lack of closeness to others experienced in childhood. In an attempt to compensate for this lack, they ask or demand too much from friendships and end up feeling disappointed and unloved.

The following case study is a typical example of the frustration and anger that is generated by this ineptness at social-interpersonal skills.

> At twenty-seven, Melissa was an attractive, assertive, sometimes aggressive, single parent who wanted desperately to make contact and establish close relationships with others. Repeatedly, she would extend herself in a supportive, caring way to potential friends who, at times, returned the support, but who for the most part were so needful themselves that they had nothing to return. When they were not able to give back, Melissa would turn angrily on herself and demand to know what was wrong with her. "Why can't I find and choose people who can accept my friendship and return some to me?", she would ask.
>
> In a way, she had the answer. Underneath the hard shell, Melissa was a sensitive, tender, caring young woman with deep needs to love and nurture. Her own needs for the intimacy of caring for another caused her to be drawn to people with an equal need to take. As she continued to give and give and not receive anything in return, she became frustrated and finally angry. Usually, at that point, she would become so upset that she would confront people with their lack of responsiveness and their failure to give back. Her angry behavior would cause them to act defensively, either by shouting back at her or rejecting her. She was correct in her

assessment of their lack, but what she could not see was that this was not intentional or reflective of her inability to be a friend. It was people's own inability to give to others and their need to take, that blocked their response to her.

Over time she was able to realize what she was doing and to choose people whom she could give to who also had the potential for returning some caring and support to her. With such people she was able to learn new social skills which for her really meant learning to communicate clearly, verbally and nonverbally, her thoughts and feelings. By choosing more appropriately, she was able to find people with whom she could practice her communication skills.

Two dynamics are actually at work here. First, is the inability to identify the type of person who could serve as a friend. This is frequently the case with grown-up abused children. They are so accustomed to taking care of parents, or others, and not getting their own needs met that they choose needful people as friends. They feel comfortable in the caretaker role, but are not satisfied because no one ever takes care of them. There is no reciprocity.

Second, they lack effective communication skills and have difficulty expressing in words their ideas and feelings. They have not learned how to ask for what they want and need from others. Thus, they feel frustrated and angry and often act in ways that are detrimental to the ends they seek.

SENSE OF HELPLESSNESS AND INABILITY TO MAKE DECISIONS

This lack of social skills, added to the other problems already discussed, leads to a sense of helplessness, of not having control of one's life. As previously noted, these former victims attribute both successes and problems to external causes. Grown-up abused children are unable to perceive themselves as capable of making decisions governing their lives.

If one looks at the second stage of development in Eriksonian theory in which the main task is to learn autonomous, self-defined behavior, one easily discerns the roots of these adult feelings of inadequacy, insecurity, and low self-esteem. This stage basically covers the age span of three to six years, and successful completion is characterized by the child's ability to gain independence and a degree of control over the environment. In order to do this a child needs self-confident, autonomous role models, and parents who can help set limits while allowing some freedom of choice to the child.

In the abusive family, the parents more often than not do not have control of their own lives. They are unable to set reasonable limits for themselves, are insecure, and have little self-confidence. They also tend to be rigid and unrealistic in setting rules and standards, and are overly punitive when the child fails to live up to the expected standard, even when these standards are unfair, irrational, or impossible for the child. Additionally, the parents are often frivolous about the standards they set. This lack of clarity related to standards further removes any posibility of control from the child's life since he or she cannot discern what behaviors or "rules" are appropriate to various situations.

Abusive parents thus place the child in one of three situations which preclude the learning of effective decision-making. In the first situation the child is placed in the position of having to make decisions without the benefit of proper guidance for generating and analyzing alternatives. Thus the child never learns that there can be an effective process for making decisions.

In the second situation parents take all decision-making power away from the child. They make decisions for the child without allowing any input into the process. They rarely, if ever, consider whether or not the expected behaviors are realistic or appropriate to the child's developmental level or individual abilities.

The third situation is perhaps the most confusing and destructive. Here the parents continually change their expectations or standards so that the child learns that behaviors chosen and acted out one day are not effective or applicable the next day since parental expectations have changed. This leads the child to believe that the choices they make and the actions they perform do not really make a difference.

All three of these scenarios promote feelings of helplessness and inadequacy in these children and reaffirm their beliefs that they can have no effect on their environment.

Social learning theorists have studied the development of learned helplessness in children and adults. Garber and Seligman (1980) aptly describe what seems to occur in the case of abused children. The child learns that certain outcomes (e.g., abuse, neglect, violence) and responses (the child's behavior) are independent occurrences. If the child believes that others can control outcomes by behaving in certain ways, but he or she cannot, either because they lack the skills or do not know the effective behaviors, the child feels personally helpless.

If this happens repeatedly, and further, if there is no apparent relationship between outcomes and the child's behaviors, the child may generalize the helplessness to other situations. This generalization also results in lowered self esteem since these children believe that others, who are perceived as more competent, are "better" than they believe themselves to be.

The learning of behaviors that reinforce helplessness creates complications, and often prevents the child from learning effective decision-making skills. Thus, these children begin with an underlying belief in their own inadequacy or incompetence in affecting their own life circumstances. Add to this a lack of parental role models to demonstrate how to make choices (mentioned above) or how to set reasonable guidelines or expectations, and one finds abused children growing up unable to identify or effectively act upon alternatives for making decisions or solving problems.

In addition, the chaotic and nonsupportive environment greatly limits opportunities for learning and practicing decision-making skills. That is, abused children tend not to receive encouragement for making decisions and when they occasionally do make a choice, parental response is inconsistent and often punitive, regardless of the rationality and appropriateness of the decision.

Thus, decision making becomes an impossible ordeal since one cannot see alternatives and "read the cues" ahead of time in order to forecast the reactions of others to the decisions. Often, the choice is to make no decision, and to simply "let things happen." Thus, the opportunity for feeling any sense of ownership or responsibility for the outcomes is lost and the feeling of helplessness and loss of control over one's life increases.

The following case study illustrates how this lack of control dynamic affected the life of one group member.

> Lauretta was a pretty, outwardly vivacious 19 year old whose father had died when she was about 11 years old. Her mother, a noncommunicative and passive woman, became even more withdrawn after her husband's death. In searching for a meaningful parental relationship, Lauretta turned to a neighbor who served initially as a surrogate father. Over time

he took advantage of her needs for closeness and sexually abused her.

Though bright and competent and able to make easy decisions related to her school work, when it came to her social life she "wandered" in and out of relationships with men as if trying to find an answer to a question she didn't quite understand. At the time she joined the group she was involved with a young man, slightly older than herself. She said she felt positive about this relationship because in the past she had been drawn to or "chosen" by men who, in her words, "were old enough to be my father." This new relationship seemed to her to be more appropriate and a statement of her growing control over her own love life.

Unfortunately, as time progressed her new boyfriend seemed to be confused and less certain about the relationship. He told Lauretta that he cared about her, but just didn't think he was ready to be totally committed to one person. Lauretta could understand and acknowledge his confusion. She was even supportive of him. After all, as she stated herself, they were both pretty young.

The issue came to a head when the boyfriend couldn't decide what to do about the relationship and laid the responsibility back on Lauretta. She responded with anger, tears, and frustration and blamed him for not "staying the same," for messing up the relationship with his confusion and honesty. When group members tried to get her to consider the various alternatives she had for making a decision about the relationship, she refused to listen. She kept repeating, "I don't know what to do. I can't make this or that decision." Her choice was to do nothing and eventually the boyfriend slowly withdrew from her. She made feeble, covert attempts at staying in touch with him and salvaging the relationship by visiting his mother and sister when he wasn't home, but could not openly come out and state or make a decision to be either committed to or separate from him.

UNRESOLVED FEELINGS

Underlying nearly all the other problems of grown-up abused children, and certainly related to the lack of trust, is an ability to identify emotions and express, or "own" one's feelings. Perhaps the most common way of handling emotions is to deny their existence. Many of these adults claim never to feel anger, resentment, hostility or their opposites such as joy, happiness, warmth, and closeness to others. Wilson (1980) and Lifton (1979) have identified similar behavior in victims of traumatic experiences and call it *psychic numbing*.

The tendency is to deny the presence of any affect. It is not unusual to hear such a person, in a tightly controlled body posture, with hands and teeth clenched, all muscles tensed, eyes flashing, insist that he or she is fine, relaxed, not at all upset. Usually the person is totally unaware of the nonverbal physical cues the body is sending. Even when these behaviors are pointed out and other people acknowledge that given similar circumstances they, too, would be outraged, the grown-up abused child will claim to be totally unmoved and experiencing no emotion at all.

The incongruity between affect and behavior is not limited only to the expression of negative emotions. Feelings of happiness are also denied or repressed. Many former abuse victims report almost no experience of joy, exhilaration, or even satisfaction.

This behavior is understandable, perhaps even predictable, given that as children these people were often punished for being too exuberant. At best, parents frowned upon and discouraged the excessive activity associated with these children's joy of accomplishment. Even as they grew older and did not express their satisfaction so boisterously, they usually found that achievements were not met with praise or reinforcement, but rather became occasions for ridicule or physical beatings designed to "put them in their place." Two lessons were learned: joy should not be expressed, or even felt; and happiness is followed by pain. The ultimate lesson was that it is best not to be happy or to express or acknowledge any emotion at all.

This belief is strengthened further by abuse victims' negative self concept and low self-esteem. They do not believe they have a *right* to feel happy or proud—or angry, for that matter; often the only emotion they will admit to feeling is guilt, which they believe they deserve to feel.

At the opposite end of the spectrum are those individuals who are so very conscious of their anger and other intense feelings that they become immobilized. They believe that if they were ever to begin to express the deep feelings of anger, resentment, and hatred, they would never be able to stop. They feel the emotion so strongly that they believe the only way to be safe is to totally suppress it, to remain rigidly, adamantly in control.

Several factors are at work in this process. First, much of the anger these people feel is directed toward their parents. They believe that such a negative reaction to the people they are "supposed" to love is inappropriate and *wrong*. Therefore, guilt moves them to repress the feelings.

Second, their experience has taught them that anger is destructive and frequently results in violence and physical beatings. Never having observed or learned other modes of expressing angry feelings, they are fearful that they may repeat the process of abuse in their own lives. Without effective alternative behaviors, the only recourse they see is to totally deny or repress the emotion.

Many of these adults tend to intellectualize their anger. They admit that it is reasonable, justified, and a realistic reaction to what they have experienced, but they feel no purpose would be served and much destruction and violence might follow were they to express it.

Others unconsciously displace their anger onto other people, situations, or things. For example, one woman who participated in peace demonstrations in Washington, D.C. in the 1970s suddenly realized as she was shouting anti-war slogans along with other demonstrators that her fierce anger and frustration was not really felt toward the U.S. government, but toward her abusive parents. This insight helped her to finally begin dealing wih her unresolved anger at her parents.

Another interesting dynamic sometimes occurs in relation to this unconscious acting out. On occasions when former victims have struck out in a violent fashion, they report that they were not aware of having any feelings of anger. Whether the violent act was directed at their parents, another person, or just some nearby object, there seemed to be no connection between any present feelings and the action being performed. In some cases there were not even any apparent precipitating events; the former victims simply performed the violent act with no reason and no identifiable accompanying affect, a generalized striking out.

One extreme example of this kind of aggression is the case of Karen.

> Karen was part of a group of radical students on a large university campus during the late 1960s when the burning of buildings as a form of protest was prevalent. She participated in the setting on fire of an ROTC building on campus. She was arrested, convicted, and actually served time in jail for this action.
>
> Years later, as a participant in our group, Karen recalled the event. While talking about her great anger and resentment toward her parents, she had suddenly remembered the apparently unrelated past event. She talked about how she had felt "driven" during her college years by an intense inner energy which she now could understand as her anger and

hostility. She told how as she helped to light the fire she felt no emotion. Instead, she said she experienced a distance from the event, almost as if she were two people — one on the outside watching dispassionately as "this person" (herself) performed the aggressive act.

The above case study incident illustrates the absence of affect frequently experienced. It seems to be almost a disassociation to the event.

In addition to anger and hostility towards others, there is fear. Many grown-up abused children want so much to be liked and to gain approval that they are afraid that everything they say or do may cause offense and result in rejection. Again, this is traceable to their never having been approved of as children; never having been rewarded; never having had the satisfaction of having an impact on their world; never having received a consistent, freely given, unconditional love. Most of what they have known is rejection.

There is often an incredible degree of compulsiveness in their effort to "do the right thing," an unrealistic desire to be perfect. They seem to believe that if only they could be perfect, they would be loved and accepted — they would not be rejected.

Finally, when one gets beyond the anger, the resentment, and the fear, what frequently shows up is a constant guilt which is reinforced by the person's belief in his or her worthlessness. If one of these adults ever admits to and expresses anger at the treatment of abusing parents, almost invariably the response will be guilt. This guilt is caused by two factors. First, they have been told that they are supposed to love their parents and that they are not allowed to be angry at them. Second, society tells them that parents act in the best interests of their children; thus, if they were mistreated, it must have been their own fault. They must have done something to "mess things up." Therefore, they have no "right" to be angry. This latter belief is generalized to others. Often, they will express guilt at having anger at other people when they are mistreated, even when the anger is justified. Occasionally, this guilt manifests itself in self-punishment and self-mutilation. At worst, it is apparent in suicide attempts.

An interesting point to note is that even in the case of an adult who has grappled with and successfully expressed anger and firmly believes this expression is justified, frequently a nagging uncertainty, a trace of guilt, remains. Most must simply learn to live with it. It is as if the belief in one's own "badness" is so thoroughly ingrained that no matter how successful one becomes or how hard one works, the internalized "fact" remains that "if only I had been better, if only there weren't something wrong with me, my parents would have loved me." Though the physical beatings may have ended, and the ties are broken so that the psychological harrassment and verbal disparagement are cut off, these adults often remain victims of their own consciences and take on the role of the abusive parent.

In the following section we discuss another issue which sometimes plagues grown-up abused children. While not classified as one of the other five recurring problems, the effects of sexual abuse on personal identity, in particular sexual identity, warrant special attention.

SEXUAL ABUSE

The degree to which sexual abuse affects the adult's sense of identity seems to be related to the age at which the abuse was experienced and to the behavioral reaction of significant persons (parents, physicians, police) in the child's world. As Leaman (1980, p. 22) states, "The parents' reaction is probably the greatest single prognostic indicator of emotional effects of an incident of sexual abuse on a child." Basically, if the parent responds with concern and caring for the child, recovery is faster and longer lasting. This assumes that the instance of abuse is made known to and believed by persons in authority. For those children who are sexually abused by a parent and whose experiences are not made known to or believed by other adults, the prognosis is not so positive.

Judith Herman (1981) discusses three research studies which consider the lasting effects of sexual abuse during childhood. According to these studies, three factors are crucial to the development of pathology in adult life, namely whether or not (1) the sexual relationship involved the use of force; (2) the relationship continued over a long time; and (3) the abuse was perpetrated by a relative or family member. Herman cites Gagnon's (1965) conclusion that victims who reported sexual contact which involved use of force or coercion, and continued over a long period of time had a high incidence of psychic damage and long-term problems in adult life.

Finkelhor (1979) confirms the finding that effects are long lasting when the abuse is forced and of long duration. He also found that men and women who had been sexually abused in childhood showed impaired functioning in what he called "sexual self-esteem" when compared to others of their age group who had not been abused.

We have found that this impaired functioning is manifested in several ways. Frequently, adults who have been victims have totally repressed all memories of sexual abuse. They may recall, and even discuss, instances of physical violence, but they will deny that they were sexually abused or will modify the experience to make it less serious. For example, they may recall having their genitals fondled by an adult, but will repress the experience of intercourse. Often, they have a seemingly irrational fear, or at best discomfort, related to hugging and kissing or other behavior which precedes sexual contact. It is as if the unconscious memory interferes and causes confusion as to what appropriate sexual behaviors are.

For those who do not repress the abusive sexual experience, Herman (1981, pp. 29-30) points out a tendency toward repeated victimization in adult life. She discusses the reports of teams of workers at two rape crisis centers in Albuquerque, New Mexico and Tacoma, Washington, who noted that 18 percent and 35 percent, respectively, of the women who had been raped had a history of incest. We have also seen this in our group: former victims of childhood sexual abuse report having been molested, beaten, or raped or have deep feelings of vulnerability and fear that they may be victimized again.

In part, these fears are evident in the great sense of isolation and alienation that these adults feel. Their struggle to establish intimate relationships is made even more difficult than it is for those who have been physically abused. Herman (1981, pp. 99-100) found this to be true in her own study of abuse victims. As she states:

> The isolation these women felt was compounded by their own difficulty in forming trusting relationships. The legacy of childhood was a feeling of having been profoundly betrayed by both parents. As a result, they came to expect abuse and disappointment in all intimate relationships . . . to be exploited . . . Given these possibilities, most women opted for exploitation.

Women in our group have reported acting out their choice of exploitation without being aware of what they were doing. These women tend to be flirtatious and almost invite sexual overtures through innuendo and suggestive comments. Psychologically, we may explain this as identification with the aggressor. Often, when these women were queried about their behavior and its motivation, what they described is a search for male approval or a willingness to be exploited, rather than a desire for sexual contact. These women also expressed some fear of the sexual experience, but somehow they had come to believe that one way to make men like them was to portray themselves as willing and eager sexual partners. Generally, they did not perceive sexual acts as mutually satisfying, but had seen them as gratifying to the man. This is not to say that these women did not enjoy sexual relations since frequently they reported that they did; however, the motivation was more toward satisfying the man's needs rather their own.

At the opposite end of the spectrum is a quite different behavior frequently manifested by adult women who have been abused as children. Instead of acting in a flirtatious manner, such women were withdrawn and anxious around men. They expressed varying degrees of fear related to developing relationships with men which might eventually result in sexual contact. What seems to have occurred is that the experience of precocious sexual contact or intercourse was so painful and frightening that, as adults, these women retained their fears and thus chose to avoid contact or close relationships with men. Often these women would express a belief that they were "tainted" or "unclean" and perceived sexual acts as being painful, frightening, or "dirty."

Occasionally, these women became so afraid of men that they identified themselves with other women and claimed a lesbian preference. Obviously, one may develop either a heterosexual or a homosexual preference for any number of reasons. Unfortunately, in the case of some women who have experienced sexual abuse, there is no real choice—they are afraid to consider the heterosexual alternative.

There seems to be similar confusion over sexual identity in some men who have had violent, abusive fathers and passive though warm and nurturing mothers. The man may identify with his mother and become effeminate or even homosexual as a way of disowning any relationship with, or similarity to, the violent, aggressive father.

Another dynamic may occur when there is an aggressive mother and passive father. In one case in our experience, a male group member acted out the trauma of sexual (coupled with physical) abuse by his mother in the opposite manner. Rather than choose an effeminate standard for behavior, he became sexually active at an early age and continued on into mid-adulthood seeking sexual encounters almost as conquests to reaffirm his own manhood and sense of control and power over his own sexual life. Most often these sexual experiences were devoid of real love. They were more a confirmation of his sexual competence and male identity and an acting out against a dominant, hostile mother rather than acts of intimacy for the purpose of gaining closeness to another person. Once this man recalled the sexual abuse and made the link to his previous experience, he was freed of the compulsion to seek out sexual conquests and able to commit himself wholly to an intimate, loving relationship with a woman.

Although we have not encountered many men with a history of sexual abuse, there is reason to believe that the frequency of this experience is greater than previously believed. Both Finkelhor (1979) and Gagnon (1965) found in their studies of nonclinical populations that 5 percent to 10 percent of all American men have been sexually victimized as children. Further, Nielsen (1983, p. 139) reports that "professionals involved in child abuse projects indicate that boys comprise 25 percent to 35 percent of their caseloads." What is clear is that boys are less likely to report these experiences for fear of personal harm or because they are afraid they will be labelled homosexual since most sexual abuse of young boys is perpetrated by an older male.

FLASHBACKS AND NIGHTMARES

One final problem that occurs frequently, especially in relation to sexual abuse, is the occurrence of flashbacks or of negative memories of violent past experiences. Often these memories are so vivid and terrifying that the adult becomes disoriented and out of touch with the here and now. Physical trembling, rapid heart beat, loss of breath, and physical pain become part of the reaction to the flashback.

These flashbacks have their unconscious counterpart, which takes the form of vivid, frightening nightmares. If the adult has long repressed the sexual abuse and begins to get in touch with the past experiences, flashbacks and nightmares may be expected to occur as part of the process of working through and attempting to resolve the experience.

Getting the person to discuss these memories is critical to helping him or her understand and gain perspective on the past. The first step is for the person to admit that the event actually occurred and to describe it or "walk through" it. Next, the person needs to identify the feeling states related to this past event. Owning the feelings and accepting them as "all right" is the third step toward gaining resolution. Finally, we continue to affirm to the person that, while we understand that they are having the flashbacks and feeling the effect associated with them, they are, in fact, present in the here and now. The past event is not really taking place. Over time the flashbacks and nightmares tend to lose some of their debilitating effects upon the person though they still remain as painful reminders.

A FRAMEWORK FOR UNDERSTANDING

At least one expert (J.P. Wilson, 1983) believes that some grown-up abused children, especially those who have been sexually abused, suffer from posttraumatic stress disorder (PTSD). According to the *Diagnostic and Statistical Manual*, Vol. III (DSM III), "the characteristic symptoms (of posttraumatic stress disorder) involve reexperiencing the traumatic event; numbing of responsiveness to or reduced involvement with, the external world" (p. 236).

Though no published research has been done on abuse victims and posttraumatic stress disorder, the descriptive symptoms parallel many of the recurring problems that plague the grown-up abused children in our groups. For example, the feelings of alienation and isolation and the inability to establish close personal relationships and identify and express emotions sound very much like aspects of another portion of the DSM III description of PTSD: "A person may complain of feeling detached or estranged from other people . . . or that the ability to feel emotions of any type, especially those associated with intimacy, tenderness, and sexuality is markedly decreased" (p. 236).

Further, many of the symptoms of excessive autonomic arousal associated with PTSD such as hyperalertness, exaggerated startle response, difficulty in falling asleep, and recurrent nightmares, have been documented in children who have experienced repeated abuse, and have also been reported as ongoing life problems by grown-up abused children. Many of these responses were learned as adaptive survival mechanisms in childhood. In adulthood these responses, which have become basically habitual and involuntary, interfere with effective functioning.

Other features of this diagnosis which seem pertinent to the problems of grown-up abused children are symptoms of depression and anxiety. Sporadic and unpredictable explosions of aggressive behavior, or fear of such a response, in reaction to minimal provocation is still another aspect of PTSD which fits the behavioral pattern manifested by some of the survivors of child abuse. In fact, the very notion of viewing these adults as survivors (many of them perceive themselves this way) strengthens the case for applying this diagnosis. It also likens them to other populations which have already been researched such as war veterans, for whom this diagnostic category is already well accepted. If we consider the experience of growing up in an environment devoid of consistent and real love, warmth, and nurturance, but filled with violence and abuse, we may be describing the ultimate trauma.

This diagnosis is useful because it allows the group leader to understand the symptom patterns as a whole system related to each person's history of abuse, and then to deal with the whole accordingly. That is, rather than singling out one or more symptoms for treatment, the leader perceives the cluster of symptoms as an interrelated pattern of response to excessive stress and trauma during the person's early development. Treating only one symptom will probably not be particularly effective and might upset the interrelated responses, causing greater discomfort rather than relief. Creating a supportive milieu through the support groups, as will be described in the following chapters, is one way of attempting to respond to the cluster of symptoms as a whole entity.

In this chapter we have attempted to summarize and provide some descriptive examples of the more typical problems or symptoms experienced by grown-up abused children. Where possible, we have traced the effects of abuse back to childhood experiences during various developmental stages. In the next chapter, we will discuss the underlying goals and structure of the support group approach to treatment.

CHAPTER TWO

GOALS AND STRATEGIES FOR SUPPORT GROUPS

THE goals of support groups for grown-up abused children are directly related to the individual and interpersonal problems discussed in the previous chapter. These group goals have been clarified over time and, like the problems or issues which they seek to address, they have been identified repeatedly by individual members as prerequisite to the achievement of individual goals.

Before we begin a discussion of these goals, a few comments need to be made about the group leaders' role in facilitating a group process that will enhance goal achievement. During the initial meetings of the group, the leaders must accomplish two tasks. The first is to create an environment that is perceived by members as being safe and comfortable enough for them to present and discuss (in as much detail as they are able) the particulars of their abuse experience. Acknowledgement and discussion of this past experience will provide a basis for the establishment of trust and sharing among group members. As we have stated, this lessens the isolation that individuals feel and assures them that their background is not unique to them. Thus, they no longer need to believe that, if they were not inherently bad, unloveable, and inferior, they would not have been abused. They can place the past experiences in perspective, recognize that they were innocent victims, and begin to disown the blame or responsibility for what happened to them.

The second task for the group leaders is to help individual members identify the specific problems that they would like to resolve.

Once these issues are identified, the leaders can encourage and help each member to establish related goals and objectives for personal growth.

In general, individual goals fit into the framework of the six basic goals for groups. These group goals relate to creating a group environment that enables individual members to achieve their own objectives and have recurred over time and across groups. Each will be discussed individually although they are not totally discrete. There is some overlap and achievement of one goal often seems prerequisite to identification of and action toward achieving another. We will list the goals here and follow with a detailed dicussion of each.

GOALS FOR GROUPS

1. To break down the sense of isolation that former abuse victims experience.
2. To provide a safe, supportive, and understanding environment in which members can share past and present experiences, express feelings, experiment with new behavior(s), and develop close personal relationships.
3. To provide a consistent, predictable environment in which members can learn that they can trust others and that they themselves are trustworthy and entitled to self-esteem.
4. To provide opportunities for group problem-solving to help members learn to make decisions and take greater control of their lives.
5. To enable and encourage members to express long repressed emotions so they can overcome the fears they have associated with the experiencing of emotions, and learn appropriate ways of expressing feelings.
6. To provide a setting in which members can learn and practice interpersonal communication skills that enable them to meet their personal needs.

Goal One

To break down the sense of isolation that former abuse victims experience.

This goal has already been touched upon in the introductory remarks, but it deserves more attention. As we have stated, grown-up abused children have rarely shared or discussed their experience of abuse with other people. This is partly because of the general lack of communication in their homes. Further, as children or adolescents, when the abuse was most severe, they were repeatedly threatened to be silent about the abusive behavior of their parents. Many were led to believe that the abuse was punishment which they deserved and received because they were "bad."

Those who finally could no longer endure the abuse or became aware that it was not a normal family interaction, and did attempt to discuss their situation with others, usually were not believed. Frequently, they received even more "abuse" from the person they had chosen to trust as confidante. They were chastised for telling "lies" about their "lovely parents." Most of the adults in our groups thus far grew up in the fifties and sixties when society did not permit discussion of child abuse or recognize it as a problem of "nice" people.

Of course we know today that child abuse is the one crime that cuts across all socioeconomic classes and racial and ethnic backgrounds. But very few persons, even mental health professionals, knew this twenty, thirty, or forty years ago when our group members were young. Outsiders to whom abused children tried to confide their experiences generally tried to deny what they were hearing and refused, or were reluctant, to become involved in other peoples' family lives. In the rare case that someone was willing to listen and wanted to provide assistance, there were few, if any, resources available to aid the abuse victim. Often, the only help he or she received was the relief felt at finally having told someone and been believed. Thus, for the most part the silence and sense of isolation were reinforced by others outside the family unit.

Thus, a large part of this goal is to get the group members to feel that it is all right to finally disclose those experiences they have carefully hidden from others all their lives. We use discussion of group goals as a tool to help make members feel comfortable enough to disclose their past experience. Repeatedly, we have seen that as soon as one person breaks the barrier of silence and begins to share the past experience, the others quickly follow, expressing relief at finally being able to "tell their stories." The extent of detail varies from person to person. Some seem to need to "play out" specific past events or memories; others speak only in the most general terms. This stage of group development rarely lasts more than one or two sessions.

The actual telling of past experiences functions as a catharsis and begins to break down the defenses that have kept these individuals insulated, as well as isolated, for most of their lives. It is a painful, difficult sharing, not a swapping of horror stories. As such it is one of the greatest risks the group members have taken in their lives. After this goal has been achieved, the taboos have been broken, and the episodes of abuse have been acknowledged by others, the former abuse victims can begin to move toward a sense of closeness to, and trust for, others and a greater understanding of themselves.

Goal Two

To provide a safe, supportive and understanding environment in which members can share past and present experiences, express feelings, experiment with new behavior(s), and develop close personal relationships.

This goal is closely related to the first because the only way to make it really possible for these adults to share the experiences of the past and break through the shells that keep them isolated from others is to provide a safe place and the opportunity and impetus to talk about painful and difficult issues. One way in which the group leaders set the stage and attempt to build the basis for trust is to begin the first group meeting with a discussion of the ground rules or guidelines that are critical to the group's success.

The first requirement is that group members agree to be active participants within the group process. Although this may seem so obvious as not to need mentioning, we have found that many abuse victims find it incredibly difficult to talk about themselves in a serious, honest manner. Most of them would like very much to be open with their feelings and free to discuss their problems, but years of experience have taught them that it is not safe to talk about those things because they become vulnerable. Thus one of the responsibilities each group member assumes is to provide encouragement and support to other members.

The group leaders must remind the members frequently that they will be encouraged, and even pushed, to disclose and explore issues and problems. One of the ground rules with respect to this "pushing" is that if a person is truly unable to talk about an issue, or if the discussion becomes too frightening or painful, the rest of the group will back off until a later time. As one group member stated very aptly, "I know I need to be on the hot seat sometimes, and I know I'll learn and grow from it, but sometimes it gets too hot and I'm afraid I'll get burned. Then I need to stop for a while." This stance seems fair to group members because they know well that unresolved issues will continue to clamor for understanding and resolution.

A second requirement relates to the need for confidentiality. Given the problems with trust that grown-up abused children experience, confidentiality is clearly a key issue requiring discussion. It has two aspects. First, group leaders must emphasize that, as in all therapeutic settings, the issues, problems, and feelings expressed and discussed in the group are not to be discussed with nongroup members.

Second, matters discussed in the group may not be discussed privately by members outside the group sessions. Occasionally, group members do meet in pairs or threesomes outside the group or phone one another for support. We strongly encourage this kind of interaction. However, if members discuss group issues, especially process issues, there is potential for such discussion to interfere with group cohesiveness.

For example, in all groups there are occasions when time runs out and issues or problems are left unresolved. This can result in a great deal of anxiety for group members—who all tend to experience intense guilt feelings if the group does not "go well." This guilt and anxiety may cause one member to call or meet with another member in an attempt to gain understanding or at least diminish the anxiety.

This discussion can be very useful if it results in resolution of a problem that has arisen in the group between these same two members. But when this occurs, we ask that at the next meeting these members share with the others some information about the resolution so that it is clear that the problem has been dealt with and no longer needs attention.

Outside discussion can also become harmful when one member has a problem with another member and, instead of dealing with that member, calls on a third member for support. The danger in this process becomes apparent at the next group meeting when two people come in and align themselves against the other. Such alliances are destructive both to the individual's growth and to the group's life. They should be discouraged. (Generally, this has not been a problem, but it deserves discussion from the outset before it occurs.) It is important to remember that such alliances occur because of the fear and incompetence a group member may feel at having to stand up to (and usually this means disagree with) another person.

We also ask that group members suggest any guidelines that they would like the group to follow. This provides impetus for a discussion of members' fears, concerns, and reservations about being part of the group. Talking about these fears and concerns tends to provide a natural lead into the discussion of the previous abuse experiences of group members. By this time they have had a chance to relax somewhat and to get used to the leaders and other group members, and many are finally ready to disclose and "unload" their past history.

Group members talk about their abuse experience in many ways. As we have said, some simply say they were physically abused by their father or mother; others go into more detail about specific past events. The degree of detail does not seem so important initially as the actual "public" statement of having been a victim of abuse. The nonverbal expressions of relief after the disclosure seem to shout. Body postures become more relaxed. Tension fades from faces. Often, group members will laugh and joke about how afraid they were to tell of their past and will express their surprise at how easy it was once they got started. Occasionally, someone will even cry.

While this display of emotion is not surprising, what seems unusual is the immediate natural empathy that seems to flow between group members. The expression of this painful common bond seems to draw the group together and begin the process of creating a safe, supportive, and understanding environment. While each person's individual abuse experience is unique, the feelings of being alone in the world and being the only one with this terrible stigma seem to fade as members realize that there are others who have been victimized and endured the shame and pain of abuse. This insight helps group members learn the process of caring and providing support over time as they get to know one another better.

Consistency becomes a key component in the successful achievement of the second goal and is the focus of the third goal. Because of the ever present chaos in the abusive home, establishing a consistent base in the lives of these grown-up abused children is a critical goal which warrants individual attention.

Goal Three

To provide a consistent, predictable environment in which members can learn that they can trust others and that they themselves are trustworthy and entitled to self esteem.

One characteristic of the abusive family that experts in he field of child abuse have observed repeatedly is the inconsistency of parental behavior. As we have said, this inconsistency and the resulting inability of abused children to predict the consequences of their own behavior are primary reasons abuse victims have great difficulty in learning to trust themselves and others. Thus we have found that it is important to stress consistency and order in the group setting.

Consistency of response, especially on the part of the group leaders, is critical. As the group progresses and members become more open to expressing fears, needs, problems, and weaknesses there is a constant need for reassurance and support. Group leaders will be tested repeatedly to see if they deviate from a consistent, supportive response. Often, this "testing" takes the form of baiting in which group members intentionally engage in regressive or other inappropriate attention getting behavior just to see how the other members and the leaders will react.

Since this behavior tends to be self-defeating, it is important to confront the person directly while at the same time providing reassurance that he or she is still likable and worthwhile. We emphasize the inappropriateness of the *behavior*, not the person. The following example will illustrate how one such instance of self-defeating behavior was handled effectively:

> Mark had been a member of two successive groups over a period of about one and one-half years. During most of this time he had rarely spoken though he had been encouraged often to participate. Finally, during the second year another group member expressed her frustration and annoyance at his reluctance to share his thoughts and feelings with the group. Something finally clicked for Mark and though hesitant, he began to offer more and more comments at each group meeting.
>
> At one meeting nearly the entire time was devoted to helping Mark with a problem he was facing. Though he was tense and nervous, he seemed to enjoy being the center of attention and was open to comments and suggestions. Toward the end of the meeting he expressed his appre-

ciation to the members and told them how helpful the session had been for him.

During the next two group meetings the focus was primarily on other group members and Mark reverted to this more typical behavior of limited verbal participation although he remained attentive and interested in the group activity. By the third week his verbal participation was limited to one- or two-word responses and his nonverbal behavior included very little or no eye contact and a lack of attention to what others said. When asked to participate, he simply replied, "Pass." It became clear that he was using this regressive behavior to manipulate the other group members into paying attention to him. Several members became angry and started confronting him with his "childish" behavior.

At this point the group leader intervened and pointed out how the behavior was self-defeating and was not helping Mark to get the positive response and attention he really wanted and needed. The leader emphasized that she understood that it was difficult for Mark to ask directly for what he wanted, but that one purpose of the group was to help members learn more effective behaviors for getting what they want or need.

She also stressed that everyone liked and cared about Mark, but that his regressive behavior was not acceptable. She encouraged Mark to take a risk, be more assertive, and ask for support instead of attempting to manipulate the other members. The other members' anger was defused and they were able to be supportive and to make sincere efforts to draw him out.

As illustrated in the above scenario, the key element is consistency in (1) providing reassurance and support and (2) in not allowing ineffective or self-defeating behaviors.

Providing structure and order is another important way to promote consistency in the group. It also serves to ease the tension and raise the comfort level of group members. To reiterate what we have already said, during the first group meeting the guidelines are spelled out and agreed upon, the content and structure of the groups are outlined, and group goals are clarified; members spend time identifying individual goals and expectations and discussing some of their experiences. Members and leaders agree upon a regular meeting time of one and one-half or, preferably, two hours per week based on individual schedules.

We initially ask group members to make a commitment to attend four consecutive meetings. This commitment is extremely important. All groups take some time to form and develop cohesion so that members feel comfortable. We have found that members need a minimum of four meetings to give the group a "fair trial." After the four meetings have passed, we discuss with group members how they feel the group is going. Modifications are made as needed, and a longer commitment of two to three months is determined. Another reassessment of group progress is done at that time.

Group leaders need to be aware of one important fact related to this commitment to attend meetings. For a grown-up abused child, the hardest part of being a group member may be coming to the meeting. For many of these adults, this is the first attempt to act counter to their past behavior of refusing to acknowledge their abuse experience. One woman, for example, came to the third meeting of a group and admitted that she had come to the first two meetings at the appointed time, but had stayed in her car the entire two hours. After each meeting, one of the group leaders had called to ask if she was still interested in participating, had told her the next week's meeting time, and encouraged her to come. Only at the third attempt could she overcome her fear and anxiety and leave her car to join the group.

Leaders must repeatedly stress that each member is important to the group process and should encourage members to contact one another the day before a meeting to ensure full attendance. This procedure also helps to hasten and strengthen the development of group cohesion.

If at any time a member decides to drop out of the group, he or she is asked to attend at least one more meeting to discuss the reasons for terminating. The most common reasons a member considers dropping out of the group are (1) anxiety, and (2) the belief that the group has not met and will not meet the person's needs or expectations.

Between group meetings members' anxiety levels can rise to such high levels that they are afraid to come to the next meeting. (Causes of this anxiety are varied and are further discussed in Chapters 3 and 4.) Usually, a member will call one of the leaders to say that he or she "can't" come to the group any more. At that point, the leader can talk through the fears, provide reassurance, and encourage the member to express the concerns at the next meeting and ask others for support. Since these fears are generally shared to a greater or lesser degree by all members, strong reassurance and much positive reinforcement for returning to the group are offered.

In the second case, that is when a member believes the group is not meeting his or her needs, a similar strategy is applied. We ask the member to return to the group and state as clearly as possible just what those needs or expectations are. The hope, of course, is that alterations can be made to accommodate individual needs.

For the most part, members' criticisms of the group process are well taken. Frequently other members will admit that the group was not fully meeting their needs or expectations, but they have been too afraid to speak up. Others may say that they have been aware of "something missing," but could not quite say what was "wrong" with the group. These discussions not only act as positive reinforcers for the group member who raises the issue but also serve to move group interaction to a deeper level. They also serve as living proof that it is safe and all right to ask for what one wants and needs, even if that means being critical. Finally, members can learn that positive, assertive behavior can be an effective means for getting what they want and need.

Another reason for having members discuss their intention to drop out of the group is to make it clear that their desire to leave is not the "fault" of any other member. Frequently, members will express guilt or fear at having said or done something in the group that they believe may have "hurt someone's feelings" or caused someone to feel "rejected." Even when a member misses a meeting because of illness, several group members will feel certain that the absent person has stayed away because of something they have said or done.

Again, it is necessary to reassure these people that their behavior was fine, that they did nothing wrong, and that they are still likable, worthwhile people. Thus, although this rule is difficult to enforce, it is worth the time and effort to encourage individuals to discuss their intentions and reasons if they are considering leaving the group.

Obviously, group members do reach a point at which the decision to end their participation is natural and healthy. They may have gained sufficient insight and no longer need additional support from the group. In general, we have found most members terminate after nine months to one year.

In our particular setting (a university campus), the meeting schedule is controlled to some degree by the schedule of the academic year. Thus, each quarter a new time is scheduled for the group meetings; this depends upon members' class schedules. Occasionally, it is impossible to find a time that accommodates all members. When this occurs, those with time conflicts are offered the option of transferring to one of the community-based groups.

While this solution is not totally satisfactory, it is better than a forced termination based on a schedule conflict. Members who have transferred to another group have reported some anxiety and trepidation about "starting over," but most can adjust rapidly and later said that the experience was not as difficult or traumatic as they had originally anticipated.

There have also been a few group members who dropped out for a quarter rather than start with a different group. They rejoined the group in a later quarter. As a substitute for participation, these members tend to seek support from the group leaders in individual weekly or bimonthly counseling sessions and frequently keep in telephone contact with the other group members. This facilitates their return to the group as regular members.

Meeting times of community-based groups tend to be more stable. Therefore, there is less member movement in and out of these groups.

Generally, each meeting starts with a brief opportunity for each person to summarize positive and negative events from the previous week in a sort of "touching base." Leaders ask members whether there are issues or concerns that they want the group to deal with that day. This helps the leaders to determine how much time may be allotted to each person and whose concerns are the most pressing and require immediate attention.

While this technique is generally very useful for providing consistency and structure to the group meeting and for having concerns expressed at the start, problems do occasionally arise. Since it is often very difficult for abuse victims to talk about problem areas or negative events in their lives, once they do manage to bring up these concerns it is also difficult to "turn them off" and "put them on hold" until later in the group meeting.

For example, one group member who had extremely hostile feelings toward her mother finally started to talk about her anger and hostility at the beginning of one session. She began to express these feelings in relation to a recent incident that had brought them to the surface. After several minutes of discussion, we felt it was necessary to go on and "touch base" with the other group members. Thus, we asked if this was something she wanted to come back to later in the meeting. She gave a begrudging "yes" and we continued around the circle.

Later, when we tried to get her to talk about her mother again, she refused. This resulted in frustration for us as well as for the other group members. When confronted with her unwillingness to share, the woman finally burst forth with anger at us and the group for not letting her finish once she had started. For her, it was too painful to "put her feelings on hold" and raise the issue twice in one meeting.

Obviously, for people like this it may be necessary to forego the usual group technique of "touching base." But, if the structure is given up and the group becomes more loose in this way, group leaders must find some other way to give each member some "air time" during the group meeting. Otherwise, the more loquacious members may monopolize the meetings.

Another concern related to the weekly reporting of events has to do with what ultimately is discussed in each group meeting. We have found that it is easy at times to fall into the pattern of discussing more current problems and putting on "bandaids" instead of moving the discussion to a deeper level where long-standing issues can be explored. While it is necessary at least to mention current problems of group members, if the discussion dwells on these the group begins to function as a crisis intervention.

A more useful strategy is to look for patterns or repetitions in members' problems and trace these to specific behaviors that were developed as defenses or survival techniques during the period of abuse. This helps to direct group discussion toward core issues such as trust or the need for control. Focusing on deeper level concerns also serves to include all members in the discussion since most can relate to the deeper issues if not to the specific event. Once members can define these issues and talk about them, they can move more effectively to change their behavior to avoid repetition of the same problems.

The first three goals we have discussed relate to the creation of conditions within the group setting which enable the group to function in a way that fosters cognitive changes in the members' belief systems and attitudes. More specifically, the premise is that once a safe, supportive, consistent environment has been established, the members will be able to explore their irrational and negative beliefs about themselves. From this will come insights which lead to greater self-acceptance and a changed attitude toward themselves and in relation to other people.

The next three goals are designed to help members use these new insights and changed attitudes to make specific changes in their behavior. These goals promote development of skills in three areas: problem-solving and decision-making, appropriate expression of emotion, and effective communication with others.

Goal Four

To provide opportunities for group problem solving to help members learn to make decisions and take greater control of their lives.

This goal relates specifically to two of the recurring problems of grown-up abuse victims which we discussed in the preceding chapter: (1) inability to generate and consider various alternative responses to problems, and (2) feelings of helplessness and lack of control. Although the goal sounds very simple and straightforward it is not so easy to achieve for it involves the use of several strategies.

First, a problem area must be chosen and clearly focused for discussion. Group members are then asked to discuss the ways in which they have tried—with varying degrees of success—to solve similar problems. As members suggest various techniques or behaviors, the leaders point out similarities in reacting to similar situations and ask which options may succeed, which may not, and why.

As the discussion progresses, the need for structure in the group again becomes evident since, as may be expected, members will frequently digress from the main issue. The main reason why these adults cannot solve problems or make decisions is that they cannot remain focused on a particular issue long enough to generate an effective solution or mode of behavior. Never having had an opportunity to generate, discuss, and implement effective responses to problems, they frequently settle on the first response that comes to mind—not always the best response—rather than consider and weigh the options.

Group discussion of alternative approaches to problem situations serves several purposes. First, it illustrates clearly that there are many ways to approach a problem or decision. Second, members have an opportunity to debate and discuss the various alternatives, and, most important, they are able to project the consequences of various actions. This second objective is essential for gaining control over one's life. As group members begin to imagine the probable success or failure of a given approach, they come to see that they do in fact have control over many of the events of their lives. They learn that certain behaviors will elicit fairly predictable responses from others — not everyone is like their inconsistent, unpredictable parents.

This knowledge or insight into one's own behavior and that of others leads to a new feeling of power and control over one's own destiny. Group members no longer perceive themselves as vulnerable, waiting victims ready to be pushed around by the actions and whims of others.

Further, as the feelings of control become stronger, the need to make choices and consider alternatives becomes more important. The thought seems to be, "Now that I believe I have some control over my life, I had better make sure I learn which decisions and actions will best help me to achieve what I want and need." Thus the group comes to help each individual to generate alternative aproaches, discuss the probable effects of those alternatives, and provide support and reinforcement for the selection of the approach which is most likely to be effective.

Even if the approach chosen does not succeed, the group can help by providing reassurance and by considering what went wrong and why. Learning to engage in this kind of logical thought pattern and to translate it into specific action is a major accomplishment for former abuse victims.

Role-playing is another effective technique for trying out different behaviors. The following example illustrates the use of this strategy.

> John, a male group member, made a decision to confront his parents with their past abusive behavior. He had struggled for a long time with the question of why they had abused him. Although he did not expect a good answer from them, he had finally reached the point where he wanted at least to tell them that he remembered what they had done to him and that he no longer wanted to keep it secret. He felt that in this way he could resolve the issue for himself to some useful degree.
>
> The group brainstormed various approaches and tried to predict the results in each case. Then two group members took on the roles of the parents while the man played himself and acted out what he would say and do. They tried several of the approaches and responses that the group had discussed. At the end of the role-playing, he said he felt ready to go

ahead and actually meet with his parents.

Several weeks later, he reported to the group that he had confronted his parents. The result was not particularly satisfactory since, as he had expected, the parents denied the past events. Still he felt good about himself for having taken the action and even found some humor in an otherwise painful situation. He recalled almost laughing during the confrontation when his real mother's astonished denial was identical to that of the "role-play" mother in the group.

This example shows how the role-playing strategy can help group members discover and practice new behaviors. This technique also provides them with vicarious experience of possible responses and prepares them psychologically for the actual event. In addition, if the real-life experience is disappointing or unsuccessful, the role-play experience has made the other group members aware of the issue and of the individual's feelings so that they can provide support and reassurance.

Finally, the group leaders have an important part to play in the group as role models. Members often find it helpful for leaders to describe their own decision-making patterns and discuss both successful and unsuccessful decisions. Members are able to see that they are not the only ones who make "wrong" or ineffective decisions: persons who were not abused are also vulnerable and make mistakes.

Goal Five

To enable and encourage members to express long repressed emotions so that they can overcome the fears associated with the experiencing of emotions and learn appropriate ways of expressing feelings.

As we have stated, at the first meeting of each group we discuss the various goals for groups. Although we explain all the goals, we especially emphasize this goal of enabling and encouraging members to express their emotions. We do this in part as a way to help members talk about their past experience of abuse. Since these experiences are filled with great emotion, members need to know that it is all right if their feelings show as they speak of these past events. We also emphasize this goal so that members know that they have the freedom to express any emotion and to say whatever they feel, even if those statements are filled with anger, hatred, or hostility. We continue to encourage this identification, acknowledgement, expression and discussion of feelings at each meeting. Frequently, a member's description of an incident from the past or present will arouse feelings of anger, pain, or guilt in other members or in the group leaders. What continues to astonish us is that often there is a complete lack of affect in the voice and nonverbal expression of the teller. Even while describing instances of brutal mistreatment or gross injustice, the person will be matter-of-fact and exhibit no affect, as if commenting on the weather. Generally the account is restricted to a simple narration. Rarely does this person express or even allude to a feeling state associated with the experience.

This obvious omission of any affect must be noted and pursued. Generally, instead of requesting the specific details of an incident beyond the information necessary to clarify what occurred, we ask, "How did you feel when this happened? How do you feel now while you're telling us about it?" The most common reply is a denial of any feeling related to the incident, or an "I don't remember." What we do notice as we ask questions about a feeling state is increasing agitation and anxiety both in the person being questioned and the other group members. As we have said in the previous chapter, what these adults learned at a very early age is that feelings are dangerous. They believe that feelings make people vulnerable to attack and pain, and that the expression of feelings, especially anger, results in violence and destruction.

The task then is to convince these individuals that they do have feelings bottled up inside them; that these feelings are natural, normal, and healthy responses to various experiences; that it is safe and acceptable to have and acknowledge feelings; and most important, that there are ways to express feelings, even anger, that are not violent or destructive. This begins with the legitimization of all feelings. When we talk about legitimizing feelings, we mean the following. We state clearly that all human beings have feelings in response to events in their lives, that these are normal and healthy responses to the environment, and that they are acceptable and allowable. We also emphasize that there are no "bad" or "good" feelings; feelings simply exist. Certainly, some feeling states may be more pleasant than others, but this is a personal assessment or valuation. What might be labeled "good" or "bad," and might result in reprisals by others is the mode of expressing one's feelings. The goal, in part, is to learn effective, satisfying, and appropriate means of expressing one's feelings. In the case of anger, nonviolent and constructive behaviors are suggested and practiced.

Group leaders generally find it most helpful to "own up to," and acknowledge publicly in the group, their own feelings about incidents they hear of or experience. We have often said to a group member who denied any affective response to the recollection of an experience that we would feel really angry or hurt or sad or whatever if we had been through that experience. Sometimes this causes great surprise on the part of the member who responds with an incredulous, "You would feel that way?"

The legitimizing of the feelings develops as other members acknowledge that they believe the member has good reason to feel that way and that having and acknowledging the feelings is all right. It is helpful to trace a natural progression of feeling reactions to hypothetical events. This provides distancing which allows the person to agree with the logic of this progression and even acknowledge that the feelings are legitimate and all right. The next step for the individual is to transfer this rational viewpoint and the legitimization of feelings to an actual experience in his or her life.

Another sort of denial can provide a major stumbling block to this process. Members end by saying, "It's all right for others to react that way, but it's not all right for me." Such statements must be challenged immediately by both leaders and members. Group members must take part in this effort because in later sessions virtually all of them will eventually try to deny that the feelings are all right for them personally; if they have helped others to claim these same feelings, the leaders can remind them of their earlier statements and point out the incongruity between their own present and past behavior. The irrationality of saying "It's all right for everyone but me" will eventually make it possible for all members to allow themselves to acknowledge and express their feelings.

Once group members begin to acknowledge the feelings they have kept pent up, or at least under tight rein, for years, the leaders need to move quickly to help them find effective ways to express these feelings. Leaders will notice that even in the case of pleasant affective states such as joy, satisfaction, or pride of accomplishment, acknowledgment and expression are tentative and guarded. One must understand that for these adults it may be hard to believe that they can laugh or express joy and not have someone ridicule or disparage them or their accomplishment. They will learn that their expressions of joy may just as readily meet with positive reinforcement, support and acclaim only after they have had many such favorable experiences.

It took one group member three years to come to finally believe that he could count on the group to be accepting and supportive of him. He tested the group many times by acting in ways that he believed would arouse anger and draw negative reactions from members. As the group continued to accept him and respond in ways that were not hurtful to him or his self esteem, he finally announced that he trusted the members and felt safe in coming to the group. He then admitted that he needed the group's support and felt comfortable with and accepted by the members. His relief at finally acknowledging and expressing his feelings toward the group was evident in both his more relaxed body posture and his increased verbal participation.

It is generally easier to encourage the expression of less explosive feelings such as joy and happiness, since people are much more comfortable with laughter, smiles, and the discussion of positive events. It is most difficult to get group members to express their anger. An initial approach to the effective expression of anger is to have members talk about ineffective, unsatisfying, or unacceptable ways in which they have attempted to deal with their anger in the past, including the denial of angry feelings and the refusal to express them.

Such discussion usually results in the logical conclusion that anger must be expressed directly because it does not go away and the price for keeping it in, such as depression or physical problems, is too high. Leaders encourage group members to raise their voices or to scream if necessary in order to express their anger and release the tension it causes. Strenuous physical exercise such as running or swimming is also suggested as an outlet for tension.

A more unusual method proved helpful to one group member.

> Darlene had an especially difficult time dealing with anger. Any time anger was discussed or expressed in the group she became visibly nervous and tense. Discussions in the group seemed to lessen her anxiety for a time, but whenever another incident occurred she would become anxious again and huddled nervously in her chair.
> Finally the male group leader moved his chair in front of hers and

asked if he could help her move out of her tense position. She nervously replied, "Yes." He helped her sit back in her chair and uncross her arms and asked her to breathe deeply. Then he held the palm of his hand open before her and said, "Darlene, please push against my hand." She looked at him in fear and said, "I can't do that. I'll hurt you." He reassured her saying, "I'm only asking you to push against it. You won't hurt me." Slowly and tentatively she began to push gently. With encouragement her effort became somewhat more forceful, but she soon stopped and said, "I can't do any more right now. It feels good, but I can't do any more today." The leader returned to his place and after a short discussion of the experience, the session ended.

In ensuing weeks other occasions of Darlene's tense response to discussions of anger arose and the same experiential opportunity was offered to her. Gradually she began to push with some force and the leader had to brace himself.

One day the leader suggested that Darlene punch at his hand rather than just push. Her initial reaction was the same anxious refusal as before but she did begin to punch gently. Over a period of weeks the force of her punches increased to the point that the group leader finally resorted to holding a pillow from one of the chairs in his hand as Darlene punched at it.

After each of these occasions Darlene had time to process the experience and discuss how it felt to exhibit her anger and then regain control. She also talked about who it was that she felt she was angry at—primarily her father.

At the end of one such session, she confided with the group, "I wish I had the courage to go over to the porno shops which are just a few blocks from campus. I understand you can buy life-sized inflatable dolls which are anatomically correct. I would like to buy one of those to pound on.

One of the other women in the group quickly responded, "What kind do you want? Male or female? I'll sew one for you."

The next week Virginia arrived pushing a baby stroller (her baby sitter was ill) and carrying a life-sized stuffed dummy over her shoulder. She had received numerous startled glances from people on the street in her walk from the parking lot.

Max, as the dummy was affectionately named by the group, was the subject of much laughter and derision as he was passed around the group. It was also discovered that under the jeans that served as his legs, he was indeed, generously anatomically correct.

After the group settled down, Darlene was encouraged to take a few jabs at Max. As with the experience before, she started very gently and very tentatively. Gradually the force and intensity increased and soon she was screaming at the dummy as she struck it.

After a time her anger was spent and Darlene collapsed in the arms of one of the group leaders. "I didn't know how angry I was at him. I now remember many more of the things he used to do to me," she sobbed. After she regained her composure Darlene looked around the room at the other group members and asked, "Are you all okay? I hope I didn't frighten you." They assured her that they were fine and that everything was all right. She had expressed her anger and no one was feeling any ill effects—except maybe poor Max.

In the weeks that followed, Darlene had other occasions to attack Max, but they gradually diminished in frequency and intensity. Although she confessed to feeling almost constantly angry immediately after the first episode, this too diminished as she gained more control over her feelings of anger. She became more able to control and focus her anger.

Most important to note in this case study is that Darlene was finally able to get her anger out in a way that was not harmful to herself or others and that allowed her to be in control of herself even while expressing intense emotion. The release of this anger also enabled her to get in touch with other emotions she felt toward her father like her great sadness and feelings of rejection. Although these were painful to deal with, she was able to work through them with the group's support and care. She also learned from this experience that others would not reject her; in fact, they repeatedly told her how much they liked and respected her. Thus her expression of emotion was positive and reinforcing at many levels.

Group members who have gotten in touch with their anger and vented it in this way have reported a qualitative difference between this conscious, directed anger and previous instances when they had "lost their temper" and lashed out violently. Even though they direct their anger only at overstuffed chairs, pillows, or dummies, they experience new awareness and control in these settings that they have not known before. Instead of striking out blindly, often at persons or things that have no overt connection with the true focus of their anger, they understand more fully what or whom they are angry with and why they are striking the object.

They are conscious of the process of their anger—its rise, climax, and gradual diminution. They also have a sense of resolution. In previous experiences of anger they often felt no real emotion and were not aware of what was happening inside them. They had never understood the connection between their angry striking out, their history of abuse and their hostility toward their parents. They had simply lashed out at whatever or whomever was closest at hand.

This physical expression of anger also has a definite cathartic effect which releases a tremendous burden of suppressed energy. Former victims report not only a relaxation of tension, but a new source of energy for other activities. They are surprised to find that after learning safe and appropriate physical means of expressing their anger (a long run or a vigorous game of racquetball) they even feel less hostile toward their parents. They are able to deal with them in a more relaxed and understanding manner.

Another way some group members are able to express their anger is to talk about the fantasies they have had related to their abusive parents. Often, these involve images of returning the physical beatings or emotional neglect they have experienced. Supportive responses to this kind of expression are essential. Leaders must be accepting and understanding of these fantasies. Group members are usually supportive because they have all had similar fantasies at some time in the past. One man admitted that at one time he had been so angry at his mother that he had tried to poison her coffee. The mother had smelled the poison and thrown the coffee away, but the man continued to carry with him an extraordinary combination of intense anger and guilt from this incident. When he finally found the courage to admit this incident to the group, he was surprised to find that members were understanding and accepting of him. Many had fantasized committing similar acts. They perceived him as a victim who had been pushed so far and abused so badly that his murderous response was understandable.

Of course, such behavior is not encouraged or condoned; murder or other physical harm to another person is not an acceptable expression of anger. But, it is essential to express compassion and empathy and to help members share that a person could feel pushed to the limits of endurance and contemplate or actually attempt such violent responses. The group responded in three ways to this man's disclosure. First, the understanding of his feelings and wishes was followed by statements indicating that the man was still liked and respected— and that he was not an "awful person" for having attempted murder. Second, the members spent a great deal of time discussing the reasons that this violent response was not helpful or effective in "really getting the anger out," and the fact that the ensuing guilt over many years had been much too great a price to pay. Third, the group discussed other, more appropriate forms of response.

We also encourage group members to express anger and guilt — not just sadness — by crying. Many of these adults admit to not having cried since they were children. At that time, tears were greeted with derision or anger by parents and became associated with vulnerability and pain by the victims. They quickly learned not to cry, and many have stated that as adults they have "forgotten" how to release their feelings in this way.

Furthermore, just as they fear expressing anger because they believe they will not be able to control it once it starts. They are afraid that once the tears start, they will be out of control and will not be able to assert themselves over the strong emotion.

The following illustrates the difficulty group members have with this type of expression.

> One young woman in particular felt a strong need and desire to cry, but she could not bring herself to the point where she could "let go." She had come to understand and accept that crying was all right and allowed. She trusted the other group members enough to allow them to see her in what she perceived as a vulnerable state. She frequently talked about wanting to cry and expressed her frustration at feeling "blocked." The boundaries finally broke down during one group meeting when she began to talk of the intense loneliness and pain she had felt as a child, her response to rejection by her mother, and her belief that she was ugly, repulsive, and totally unloveable.
>
> Her first tears were not a dramatic gushing forth, but rather a few painful, heartfelt sobs that were quickly brought in check. It was as if she were trying out the behavior to see how it felt and to see if she could regain control. Over several months, alone and in the group, she gradually became able to use the release of tears to relieve the tension and pain inside her.

No matter what form of expression is selected, the support, assurance, and reinforcement given by other members and by group leaders are instrumental in helping the person to internalize and believe in the importance of expressing emotions and continuing to strive for effective ways of dealing with them. It is important for the group to regularly discuss alternative methods and find opportunities for practicing them.

Goal Six

To provide a setting in which members can learn and practice interpersonal communication skills that enable them to meet their personal needs.

Probably the most frequent complaint from group members is that they do not know how to make friends or talk to people. They say that they feel uncomfortable and anxious in social situations. They stumble over their words and say things they do not really mean. At worst, they become so immobilized that they cannot speak at all and eventually flee from the situation.

One quiet, soft-spoken young man comes to mind. At one of the initial group meetings where members were stating their individual goals, he finally spoke up and indicated his strong desire to learn good, effective communication skills. He recalled a home life with a strict, authoritarian father who knew little English and spoke to the children only when he was angry or was disciplining them. The young man's mother had died when he was young, and the other children were equally nonverbal.

Although the specifics of his family background are different from those of other grown-up abuse victims, this home situation in which regular conversation or communication patterns are not learned or practiced is fairly typical. This deficiency in the home life makes it difficult for children to communicate with their peers and teachers at school and they often become quiet and extremely introverted. This behavior persists in adulthood.

The first step in learning new social behaviors is to admit the problem. We usually encourage group members to talk about particularly vivid memories of situations in which they felt afraid or socially incompetent. We ask for examples of the ways they usually behaved in social settings. What generally happens is that members are surprised at the similarity of their experiences. They express disbelief at others' feelings of awkwardness since they frequently perceive each other as being adept at social interaction.

This recognition that others have the same uncomfortable and anxious feelings is an important insight. Especially useful is the group leaders' acknowledgment that they also get the jitters or feel nervous in certain social situations or when meeting new people. These discussions often conclude with members laughing at their own escapades and "social failures." This serves to release the tension and helps them get to the point of discussing new ways of behaving.

We also ask group members to discuss events and situations that they expect to encounter in the near future especially those in which they will need effective interpersonal skills, such as applying for a job, going to class, and attending parties. It is helpful to have them fantasize what that situation will be like. We ask them to describe the setting, and tell the group how they intend to behave, how they expect to feel in that situation, and how they anticipate others will react. We also ask them to tell what they believe others will think or feel about them in the situation. This type of fantasizing about an expected experience in real life allows members to consider alternative forms of behavior before the event itself.

There is an important reason for having group members discuss the way they believe others perceive them. Because they have such strong feelings of inadequacy and low self-esteem, they often believe that others share their negative perceptions. Only if they are made to talk about these perceptions and the opinions they attribute to others can they question the validity of their own assumptions and see themselves more realistically.

The following case study illustrates this point.

> One male group member had decided to apply for a scholarship to cover the cost of some special training he needed. David had an initial interview with the financial aid officer and completed all the necessary paperwork. The official told him that the decision would take approximately two weeks. He enlisted the support of the two group leaders as references. They wrote and sent their letters, and the whole group waited eagerly for the response.
>
> When no notification was forthcoming after two weeks, David called to inquire about the grant. He was told that the institution was behind schedule in the processing of financial aid applications and that a decision had not been made. This continued for two weeks.
>
> At this point David scheduled another meeting with the financial aid officer. Prior to going to this meeting, one of the group leaders had an opportunity to talk with him. He was already feeling disappointed and certain that his application would be rejected. When the leader asked him why he was so sure of this he said, "The woman doesn't like me." He had no documentation or rational reason for this belief.
>
> The leader and David spent a great deal of time going over his previous contact with the aid office, analyzing both the interview and the subsequent telephone contact. Nothing in her demeanor or her verbal responses suggested that she did not like him. The leader offered several possible explanations for the officer's behavior, trying to show him that he had not necessarily been the cause of any negative affect she might have exhibited. David would say, for example, "She doesn't return my calls right away" or "She seemed like she wanted the interview to be over" as

evidence that the officer did not like him. The leader pointed out that the aid officer probably was very busy, especially if they were behind in their work, and that she had, in fact, called back.

Further, the leader agreed that it was possible that the aid officer had wanted to close the interview, but the reason could as easily have been that she had a lot of work to do, or may have felt tired or harassed that day or was in trouble with her boss. The point was to convince David that since he had done nothing to make the officer dislike him and since his behavior had been completely appropriate, there was no logical reason to assume that she had negative feelings toward him.

This case study clearly illustrates several misbeliefs that grown-up abused children hold about themselves. Quite often the reason these people experience such great anxiety in social or other interpersonal situations is that they falsely attribute their own negative views of themselves to other people. Discussion of these misperceptions is generally useful in allaying some of the anxiety. If the members can be convinced, or at least come to believe to some degree, that not everyone thinks they are stupid and that people do not make immediate judgments about their character on the basis of a first meeting, they can enter into such situations with greater self-confidence.

We also have the members share their impressions of one another. When they hear repeatedly that other people are "just like me" and feel the same incompetence and anxiety, they finally begin to believe it. This is especially true when they hear others whom they like and respect, and perceive as being relaxed and comfortable, admit that they feel nervous and inadequate in interpersonal situations.

As members gain insight into their false beliefs and begin to feel a bit more comfortable and self-confident, they can actually practice alternative types of behavior. Role-playing is very useful at this point. We generally have a group member imagine and talk about an upcoming event or situation. We ask this person to describe his or her feelings about the event and to suggest how he or she will behave. Then we hypothesize what the other person's response will be. It is usually not the response desired, so we spend some time in the group thinking of alternate ways of behaving that may achieve the desired response. Several new behaviors are selected and the group member is asked to act out those behaviors with the help of other group members. The "main character" determines all the roles and tells others how to behave, thus describing typical behavior of others in his or her life. This process provides group members with additional information about the member on whom attention is focused and with another look at that member's beliefs about others' perceptions.

Role-playing like this is particularly helpful with these adults since it provides practice in what to say and how to act in initiating contact with others. Generally, once they receive a positive response, their self-confidence increases and they begin to relax enough so a conversation can flow. Getting over the obstacle of making contact is the most difficult step.

The next step in this process is to make homework assignments — to have members try the new behavior outside the group in situations that they have imagined and discussed. Members are asked to report back to the group on how the interaction went and how they felt at the time. This process serves several purposes: members share their experiences, try new behaviors, are encouraged to talk about their feelings, and receive support and reassurance even when the attempts are successful. They receive encouragement to try again and alternative behaviors are suggested and practiced. Even a terrible "failure" can have a very positive ending when the individual receives empathy, support, and positive affirmations of his or her character from group members who freely express their caring and concern.

CONCLUSION

As is readily apparent, the goals, just like the problems which they seek to address, are interrelated and achievement of one is contingent upon progress made on another. They vary in importance throughout the group sessions as certain issues become more or less pressing. The pursuit of goals is often as therapeutic and helpful as the actual attainment, since many of these adults have never really defined or set goals for their personal or interpersonal life. Besides the resistance which can be expected, these persons manifest untiring enthusiasm and desire to attempt to overcome their past and make their future lives happier and more satisfying.

CHAPTER THREE

THE GROWN-UP ABUSED CHILD IN THE GROUP

AS we noted in the introduction, a major reason for attempting a group approach to treatment for grown-up abused children was to break the circle of isolation which has developed as a result of their abusive experience. All who have participated in the support groups, even though they initially joined with a certain uneasy eagerness, have identified the breaking down of isolation as a major advantage for them. The opportunity to finally disrupt a lifelong pattern of hiding a supposedly embarrassing fact produced a great sense of relief. Members of these groups have been remarkably faithful to the group for long periods of time (six to thirteen months) and have exhibited amazing levels of trustful sharing about their abuse, especially in view of previous patterns.

ADVANTAGES OF GROUP TREATMENT

The Reality Factor

Although the common bond which the members experience is an important aspect of the group process for grown-up abused children, several other advantages to the group approach soon become evident. A principal advantage might be called the reality factor. When persons with similar abusive backgrounds gather together to share their experiences, they achieve a realization about the commonality of their experience that they cannot acquire by reading books about child abuse.

A male group member once exemplified this very poignantly. Properly dressed in a gray business suit, he sat quietly through several group members' introductions. When his turn came, tears welled in his eyes and he said, "I'm ashamed to say this, but I'm very glad to hear what people have been saying. I don't mean that I am happy about what happened to you or about the difficulties you are experiencing, but I can't tell you what a relief it is to know I'm not the only one this kind of thing happened to, and I'm not the only one having some of the problems you all have mentioned. And you all seem quite nice. Maybe there's some hope for me after all."

The statistics about the pervasiveness of abuse in our society become real and group members finally feel that they are not the only persons to whom this has happened. They find solace in the similarities of their experiences. They begin to sense that they are not as evil as they had believed because the same things have happened to someone else who seems to be a good person. Kee MacFarlene, presently with Children's Institute International, once told of the great relief experienced by a former abuse victim whose parents had traded him for a horse when he met another person who had been traded for a dog. This person was then able to accept himself and work for his own growth in a way he had never been able to do before.

The reality factor also enables group members to be accepting of one another. Because of their common backgrounds they are able to listen to one another without the reactions of horror or disbelief with which friends or even counselors frequently greeted their accounts. No one in the group will dispute the reality of the experience or be so shocked as to be unable to offer comfort. Even the most gruesome accounts are listened to with nods of understanding and acceptance. Instead of having to prove, defend, or interpret the experience, the former victim can move directly to confronting their present personal problems which have resulted from it.

The reality factor has an important impact on the first meeting of any group. Although the first session understandably begins with a lot of hesitation and nervousness, after the first brave member shares something of his or her abusive background, others, with a great sense of relief, quickly follow suit. The depth of sharing, of course, varies from person to person, but once the process has started, no one has ever failed to acknowledge some aspect of their experience which they have never discussed with anyone before.

Many new group leaders approach their first meeting with a great deal of concern. They wonder how they will get the group to start and whether there will be enough material to keep the meeting going for two hours. Once the leaders introduce the purpose of the group and reiterate the fact that former abuse experiences are the one thing that everyone has in common, all it takes is one person brave enough to start the process. The only problem thereafter is controlling individual revelations so that everyone has a chance to speak during the two hours.

Repeatedly, new leaders report their amazement at the amount and depth of sharing which takes place in the first meeting. This, we believe, is a product of the reality factor. No group process technique can encourage sharing as much as the assurance that one is going to be fully understood and accepted.

Once the group moves beyond the point of simply sharing past experiences and starts dealing with present problems (usually by the third session), we have found that group members are also more able to acknowledge the value of help offered. The same is true of challenges for change. When either of these items come from a group of persons who have had similar experiences, they seem to have greater impact. "Maybe that suggestion can really be helpful since it comes from someone who knows what I have experienced." "Maybe I can accomplish that change since someone who has gone through the same things I have has already accomplished it."

Over and over again, it has been the pressure or encouragement from other group members which has moved a member to action when the repeated urging of a group leader has failed to accomplish the same purpose. The same words of encouragement, the same suggested solutions or approaches to a problem suddenly have a different significance, are heard in a new way, and are applied when they come from a group member who has struggled with the same difficulty.

The recognition of success can also be more real within a group of peers. "Maybe that accomplishment is significant, if the members of my group think it is"; "At last, someone recognizes how difficult it is to accomplish that one little task."

Finally, we have found that the reality factor has a feedback loop impact on participants. As one group member helps another achieve some new insight, that same understanding may have personal meaning to the originator of the idea. "I just told him that he couldn't be responsible for what happened because he was only six years old when it happened. I was only five when a similar thing happened to me." Time and time again group members have stopped in the middle of an eloquent dissertation on a recommended behavior or attitude change for someone else. With a sheepish grin they mumble: "I guess I should really follow my own advice."

Often the reality factor works as a positive form of "catch 22." Members catch each other with their own advice. "You are now telling me the same thing the whole group has been telling you for weeks. Let's make a deal. if you will follow your own advice and try _____, I'll do the same. We can report at the next meeting how it went."

Safe Environment

There are other major advantages of a group approach to treatment for grown-up abused children which, although discussed in detail in chapter two, should be highlighted here. The first such advantage is that it provides them with the safe, supportive environment which most of them have never experienced. In many ways the group provides the kind of family or community experience which the former abuse victim has always sought. The safe, supportive atmosphere fosters opportunities for the individual to experiment with and learn new behaviors without fear of retaliation. Beliefs can be analyzed without ridicule and defense mechanisms necessary in their home environment can be reevaluated for their appropriateness to the rest of the society. Interactions with this new, supportive environment are critical to improving one's self-image.

One example which highlights the impact of a supportive environment involves a very soft-spoken member of a group.

> Because he was so soft spoken, John was frequently asked by other members to speak louder and repeat himself. This often seemed to upset him and cause him to withdraw. When questioned about the behavior, he became angry and accused the group of being just like his parents who always ridiculed the way he talked and made fun of him for not talking. The group pointed out they were not ridiculing, they really wanted to hear what he had to say. In order for them to do that, he had to speak louder.

John finally admitted he had not spoken until he was four years old. His family frequently derided him for this; therefore, any comment about his speech was associated with his family. After some discussion, John was able to realize that other people could ask him to speak up and not be mocking him.

The group then became for John what his family had never been: a supportive community which encouraged him to express himself and develop his ideas. He now had a place where he felt comfortable speaking up.

Arenas for Practice

This example brings us to the second advantage of a group approach to treatment over an individual approach—that the group setting provides an arena for the former victim to practice interpersonal communication skills. Participation in group discussions and problem solving efforts naturally provides experience in the dialogue and give-and-take involved in normal conversational opportunities which their family life failed to provide. The members also learn to express their views before at least a small group of people—a new and important step for most of them.

Frequently, members use the group as an opportunity to do a "practice run" on a presentation they are going to make or a discussion they plan to have with a friend or family member. They request time to talk about the content of their proposed discussion or to role play it. Sometimes they simply ask for some words of support and encouragement before they embark on what for most people would be a very ordinary discussion.

COMPLICATIONS IN GROUP TREATMENT

Despite these advantages of group support for the treatment of grown-up abused children (and they are significant), there are complications which can arise as a result of the dynamics created by abuse. These complications, which can have a critical impact on the success of the group process, arise because former abuse victims do not react in a group the way persons from "normal" childhood experiences usually act. Former victims have learned some distinctive survival patterns and defense mechanisms. These constitute survival skills which were essential and highly adaptive in their family setting.

They are, however, maladaptive outside that setting and can short-circuit the effective workings not only of group process but also of daily living and communication. Group leaders must be aware of these distinctive characteristics so that they can move the group beyond potential break-down to individual and group healing. These factors will be examined in this section.

Distorted Communication

As we noted in Chapter One, the communication patterns of former victims have often been distorted by the abusive environment in which they lived. They learned at an early age to hide, mask, and even deny feelings and needs.

Although the group members are no longer in their family setting, the negative messages and instinctive defense reactions are still very much a part of their lives. Even if the members know intellectually that they should react differently in this setting, their instinctive reaction is to fall back on previous behavior patterns. As with the example of soft-spoken John, they know that they are not dealing with their parents and that they are free in the group to express their feelings, but that does not come easily or naturally. Their instinctive response is to withdraw or to deny their own emotions.

This is especially true whenever anger is expressed, disagreements arise, or criticism is offered. These instinctive patterns immediately reappear. Members become fearful and withdrawn. Discussions come to a frightened halt. Such experiences are distressfully similar to the situations which triggered violent episodes in their families. They are not fully able to distinguish the circumstances.

Passive-aggressive methods of communication are also common in these groups. It is difficult to elicit explicit statements of needs and desires. Members prefer not to state their wishes rather than to make a request which may be ignored, rejected, or ridiculed. Often particular members complain that the leaders or the group members are not paying enough attention to them, but this comes only after long periods of silence or minimal participation. It is only after special efforts are made to draw a person out that the group member complains that he or she has felt ignored. At other times members request help at the very end of a meeting when there is not adequate time to deal with the issue.

Joan was particularly adept at this distortion of communication. Many times she would sit quietly through a whole meeting; then, as time was running out, would bring up an important issue. Because of previous commitments, people had to leave and the topic would be postponed.

At the next meeting she would be asked at the very beginning to introduce her concern again. Responses were varied: Sometimes she would respond with anger, saying that it was now too late to do anything about it; other times she would simply say that the issue was no longer important and that it was not necessary to talk about it anymore.

The group members found this very frustrating and tried several methods to deal with this recurring problem. They tried to anticipate the problem by asking Joan early in sessions to state any concerns she might have. Often she would say she had nothing important and then proceed to drop another "bomb" at the end of the meeting. Other times she would ask to wait until later saying that it took her a while to feel comfortable enough to share. This necessitated frequent "checking back" to see if she was ready. Some meetings she would finally state her concerns in time to deal with them. Other times she would not.

The group also held long, rational discussions with Joan about why people had to leave at the time appointed for the end of meetings and why concerns needed to be brought up earlier. Some of the discussions also focused on the self-defeating nature of Joan's communication process and why she needed to overcome her fear of sharing and hasten the time when she felt comfortable. Group members assured her over and over again that they really did want to discuss her concerns and that they would take them seriously if they were given enough time to do so. They pointed out that her habit of waiting until it was too late to deal with the issue may have worked as a defense with her family, because by not giving them enough time to discuss the issue she also did not give them time to ridicule and reject her, but she did not need that defense with the group.

On occasion the discussions got emotional as group members became increasingly frustrated whenever Joan would "do it to them again." They clearly recognized the manipulative nature of Joan's process and became tired of the "guilt trip" this process worked on them.

No single event or discussion ever completely reformed Joan's behavior. She did gradually become more open and forthright about her needs and concerns. She would even on occasion state early in a meeting, "I have something I need to talk about. Will you help me talk about it?" But the process was always slow and painful. It often seemed that the group spent more time talking about why something should be discussed than actually talking about the issue. Nonetheless, Joan did learn to state some of her needs and ask for help with her problems.

Although Joan may have taken more time than most people to learn to discuss her concerns, the resistance she exhibited is not uncommon. Most grown-up abused children experience great fear and anxiety when sharing their feelings. Therefore, gentle encouragement is very important as group members make their first tentative attempts to share their feelings and experiences. Great sensitivity and much assistance with understanding, expression, and interpretation are necessary as members get back in touch with their own needs, learn to state them, and seek their fulfillment.

When communication does finally begin to take place, it may have other effects on the group process. Most freqently it is an informing and liberating experience for other members. However, sometimes one person's sharing of a past experience may trigger recollections or even flashbacks of blocked experiences for another person.

Such flashbacks, which we discussed at greater length in Chapter One, can be very powerful and disconcerting for someone who has successfully denied the experience for many years. Therefore, group leaders must be constantly vigilant about what is happening to all the members of the group. They must be alert enough to recognize the symptoms of the flashback process and sensitive enough to provide understanding and support. This will be discussed further in Chapter Four. These experiences, of course, create yet another disruption in the process of the group's life.

Sensitivity as a Defense Mechanism

Despite communication problems, one of the most distinctive features of the several grown-up abused children groups is that the initial formation process moves quickly and smoothly. The membership, of course, is self-selected, and once the participants have identified themselves as former victims and overcome their initial anxiety about participating in such a group, they are eager to get on with the task. As we have noted, the members experience a great deal of relief at finally being able to share their abusive experiences and be understood.

This opportunity to break out of their isolation and share with persons with similar experiences creates a profound sense of belonging they have never experienced before. The group becomes an oasis in their lives. This sense of community creates a strong bond of loyalty. This bond is further enhanced by the fact that the group members also exhibit an unusually high level of sensitivity and an ability to understand the feelings and emotions of the other members of the group.

The group formation and bonding process is, therefore, accomplished very quickly.

The above is an accurate description of the initial meetings of a grown-up abused children's group. The group members are very sincere about the importance of the group for them and about their concern for one another. However, because of the dynamics of abuse, these initial experiences are deceptive. Even this high level of sensitivity and understanding is motivated by the same fear and distrust that has ruled their lives for so long. These motives still guide their lives no matter how hard they try to control them.

While a certain amount of defensiveness is prevalent, and may even be proper in our society, their defensiveness extends far beyond what is normal and appropriate. It influences all their interpersonal relationships and their behaviors. Fear and distrust even influence their interpersonal sensitivity.

The former abuse victim's ability to be sensitive to the moods and emotions of others is highly developed. In fact, it operates at a level which makes those of us who have worked with these groups envious. They seem to read the feelings of other group members and the leaders as soon as they walk in the door.

> On one occasion while we were processing the previous group session, my co-leader confessed that she had had a particularly bad day before the previous meeting. She wondered whether I had been aware of it and whether I thought the group members had noticed any changes in her behavior. I acknowledged being vaguely conscious of her tension but assured her that the group would not have observed it. "It was not that evident."
>
> To the surprise of both of us, that was the first item the group members brought up. Some of them had met for coffee in the intervening week and had shared the fact that they feared that one of the leaders might have been upset with them. They were relieved to discover that the feeling was mutual; therefore, not directed at any of them personally. Reinforced by their mutual perception, they were emboldened to raise it in the meeting.
>
> My co-leader immediately acknowledged and explained her feelings at the previous meeting. The ensuing discussion revealed the acuteness of the group members' powers of observation. They easily identified several telltale behaviors which had been clues to my co-leader's tension. Many of them I myself had missed.

This incident highlights how well developed the perceptions of former abuse victims are. However, we must remember that this finely tuned skill was developed for protective purposes and that is the motivation which continues to trigger it.

As highly developed as this praiseworthy skill is for former abuse victims, we must remember that it was developed for protective purposes. In their childhood, this ability to recognize the moods of their parents was an essential survival skill. To avoid abuse they had to be constantly alert to how their abusive parent might be feeling. Thus the interpersonal sensitivity exhibited by the group members is really a defense mechanism rather than a tool for interpersonal contact and intimacy. Of course, this tendency is subconscious and group members are not aware that they are avoiding intimate relationships.

Nevertheless, the defensive character of their sensitivity hampers their ability to respond to the very feelings they identify. When any negative feelings (anger, sorrow) are recognized, the process of communication comes to a sudden halt. Causes are not explored, motives are not discussed, and methods for resolution are not considered. No method for dealing with these feelings, other than withdrawal, is considered possible. This, of course, quickly belies the effectiveness of the group bonding process. Despite the early sense of community cohesion, the underlying fear continues to paralyze members as they attempt to capitalize on the bond they have developed. Even their best intentions are sometimes thwarted by their inbred distrust.

The group setting can be helpful in dealing with this unconscious motivation. The process can be made clear and their sensitivity skills can be made to serve as means for deepening relationships rather than warding them off. Members can learn to assist one another in working through negative feelings in a constructive way. Thus they learn that negative feelings do not necessarily lead to violent and hurtful behavior. They realize that people can be helped through bad times and that relationships can be deepened by such a process.

The incident just recounted revealed all of these things and more. During the discussion which followed the initial raising of the issue, the group members not only learned that they could constructively confront "negative" feelings in another person; they also discovered that such feelings could be discussed and resolved calmly and nonviolently. They also learned that "healthy" people experience tension and negative feelings. They were amazed to find that the group leaders, whom they respected, had problems and needs which required resolution and that they could be helpful to them. Finally, they learned that they could deal with the group leaders as equals, that people supposedly in authority were willing and able to share feelings with them.

This highly developed sensitivity to the moods and wishes of others can also have a negative impact on the self-revelation process of members of the group. Their abusive experience taught them to be keenly aware of and responsive to even the unspoken expectations of the people around them. Their preoccupation with the need to recognize and respond to the preferences of others as a means of self protection not only makes it difficult for them to reveal their own needs and preferences; it also makes it difficult for them to even identify their own expectations. Their family experience taught them it was essential for self-preservation to focus on the needs and expectations of others. This strengthens their ability to be helpful, supportive, and nurturing to others in the group, but they never learn to identify and meet their own needs.

If as children they did learn to recognize their own needs and to state them to their parents, they often experienced denial, ridicule, rejection, or punishment. They were made to feel guilty for such selfishness. Soon such desires were not even allowed to reach the conscious level. The guilt was too painful.

This pain continues into adulthood. Over and over again it has happened that when group members finally allow personal needs to break through and be acknowledged, they suddenly stop themselves short. They immediately ask, "Is it all right for me to want this?" "Isn't it wrong to ask for this?" "Are you sure this is OK?" They cannot believe that they are entitled to commonly accepted forms of care and nurture. They find it hard to accept that they have a right not only to have certain feelings but also to the fulfillment of the needs which they may feel. Too often their feelings and desires have been rejected or punished.

Because of these experiences and their resultant effect on present behaviors, the self-revelation process in the group context is short-circuited at many different points. This breakdown in the flow of data about needs and expectations within the group negatively influences the group's ability to provide meaningful acceptance to members and for the members to feel accepted. When members have not fully revealed their personal needs and desires, the other members cannot take those factors into account in dealing with those individuals. Those persons then, quite correctly, feel they are not fully accepted by the group. All of this makes realistic and meaningful goal formulation difficult both for individual members and for the group as a whole.

The Acceptance of Acceptance

As we discussed previously, grown-up abused children have very low self-esteem and a profound sense of personal inadequacy. This quite naturally affects the individual member's ability to believe that the other members of the group truly accept and care for them. Despite the affinity that exists between group members and the sense of belonging that evolves from their common past, individual members still have difficulty being convinced that others accept them. This grows out of both the individual's inability to truly identify and express his or her own goals, aspirations, and needs as well as the ingrained conviction that he or she is worthless and unloveable. Constant expressions of reassurance are necessary from the leaders as well as the members of the group.

As any member shares a past experience or a past or present feeling (negative or positive) with the group, it is important to take time to reaffirm that member's acceptance. In the past, the expression of unacceptable feelings often produced abuse. Also, the sharing of abuse experiences frequently triggered avoidance on the part of others because of horror or disbelief. That expectation of rejection carries over even into a group formed specifically for persons with similar abuse experiences.

In the beginning stages of any new group, personal sharing and disclosure elicit fear and anxiety. Our experience indicates that these feelings are especially strong for grown-up abused children. In the time between the first two meetings, many members have second thoughts about what they said, whether it was appropriate, and whether they expressed themselves correctly. Their fears about acceptance become magnified and many times the discussion in the second meeting is harder to start and maintain than the first.

As group leaders, we take time at the end of the first meeting to discuss the possibility of this reaction and to assure the members that it is quite natural. We encourage members to feel free to contact us between meetings to discuss their fears. For those who seem particularly anxious, we may initiate the contact during the week. We also contact people who fail to return for the second meeting.

The same process of affirming the acceptance of members may become necessary at various times during the life of a group whenever new, particularly difficult information is shared. Even though members feel accepted by their peers and the group leaders, they often feel certain that a new revelation has destroyed their acceptance by the group. On more than one occasion members who have attended a group regularly for several months suddenly miss several meetings in a row. Inquiries reveal that they stopped coming because they were embarrassed by some new disclosure and are sure the group would not want them back. The expectation of rejection is deeply ingrained.

The group members' expectations of rejection also create much suspicion and concern about motives and consistency. Everyone in the group is subject to testing and evaluation, but most especially group leaders because of their authority position. The constant fear, even expectation, is that the leaders, like their parents, will find something wrong with them and will punish or reject them. Group members constantly watch the group leaders for signs of approval or disapproval. Over and over again group members turn to the leaders to receive assurance and affirmation for what they say or do.

Even when such approval is given, its sincerity and constancy may be doubted. Many times we have found members resurrecting issues and concerns which we thought had been dealt with and laid to rest weeks before. They return to the topic to make sure we still approve of their action, to make sure we have not changed our minds. Usually the resurrection of former topics is not done directly but slipped into the middle of some other discussion with some slight variation on the original theme. It almost seems that the attempt is to see whether, if the question is asked in a slightly different way, a different answer will be forthcoming. It should be understood that this often annoying and disruptive tendency stems from two aspects of grown-up abused children's past experience. First, they seldom if ever received approval for what they did. They cannot believe that someone is really telling them that what they are doing is fine. Therefore, they need to be constantly reassured.

Second, even if their actions were sanctioned by their family, the continuance of such approval was not guaranteed. What was encouraged at one moment might be ridiculed at another time. Therefore, they need to frequently check back to see if the approval continues. For them an issue is never completely resolved.

Comfort with Chaos

This inconsistency in past parental response also has an impact on the development of grown-up abused children groups. Chaos and unpredictability are often the standard modes of operating in abusive homes. Besides the evident chaos of a violent outburst, many other subtle forms exist. Family roles are usually ill-defined, inconsistently applied, or totally reversed. Parents fluctuate from being extremely passive, dependent persons needing to be cared for by their children to being over-bearing, violent dictators of their household. Parental expectations for their children range from normal household tasks and appropriate childhood behaviors to responsibilities far beyond their young abilities.

When they are unable to fulfill these often contradictory expectations, abuse results. The only consistent role the child learns to identify is that of the family scapegoat. Beyond that, chaos and confusion become the norm for interpersonal relationships and communication. Group members, therefore, find it extremely difficult to identify and accept roles for themselves in a group. They find it difficult to focus their attention on any one topic or person or to be the focus of the group's attention themselves. In their families, parental attention was focused only through an act of violence. Therefore, they are much more at ease with dispersed and frequently shifting attention. They are more comfortable with chaos than with structure, order, and focus.

The past chaos of their family life makes control of their environment seem impossible for grown-up abused children. They were never able to easily influence their environment; therefore, they learned early to develop passive-aggressive means of control and communication. The means of manipulation range from silence and withdrawal to incessant talking about unconnected issues.

In order to counteract these problems resulting from the group members' chaotic pasts, it is important, especially in the early stages of the group, to have a fairly rigid structure and process. This serves as a learning experience so group members can learn to feel comfortable in a controlled and controllable environment. It also assures that each person gets adequate air time, topics are adhered to, issues are brought to conclusion, and tasks get accomplished. All of these are important experiences for group members who need to develop a sense of control over their environment, which in turn provides a sense of accomplishment and self-esteem.

This factor also means that the most constant and demanding role for group leaders is that of keeping the group focused on a particular topic until it is concluded. All too frequently, members will very deftly change the subject before anything is settled. They do this either to get the pressure off themselves when they are being pushed to make a decision or to rescue someone else from such pressure. Because of their past experience, they fear that such pressure may turn hostile or that even if a decision or resolution is reached it will be considered wrong by someone, therefore result in verbal or physical abuse. They think the best course of action is to change the subject before the discussion gets to either of those two possibilities.

Group leaders must frequently intervene to point out that a topic has not been concluded or a decision has not been reached and gently but firmly refocus the discussion. Even though group members may initially complain about the rigid structure of the group, they gradually come to appreciate its importance. They soon realize that only by experiencing conclusions and making decisions which are affirmed rather than ridiculed will they, as grown-up abused children, learn that they can, in fact, make good decisions.

Goal Setting

Despite these difficulties, the group does form, esprit de corps develops, members establish relationships, and communication does take place. The group members do get down to the business of defining roles and establishing personal and group goals. However, even here abuse dynamics are at work and have an influence.

Members often have difficulty establishing meaningful and realistic goals for themselves or for the group. On the one hand, they may be evasive about determining anything specific; on the other hand, they tend to set idealistic and unattainable goals. We believe certain dynamics from their abusive pasts contribute to this problem with goal setting.

Children in abusive environments receive little or no assistance with goal setting. Their parents either did not know how to do it themselves so they could not offer training and guidance, or they simply ignored their children and left them to their own devices. Whatever the reason, the children do not learn what is or can realistically be expected of them. They flounder through their childhood and into adult life with a poorly defined sense of direction and purpose and no tools to help them make effective decisions.

A second group of grown-up abused children do not know how to set goals for themselves because they were never allowed to do so. Their parents did it all for them. These parents told their children exactly what to do, how to do it and when to do it. The children never were consulted about the goals set for them or allowed to make any decisions for themselves. Therefore, they lack the practical experience necessary to develop good decision-making skills.

Within this second set of grown-up abused children an additional dynamic is at work. Usually the goals set for them by their parents were unrealistic or inconsistent. The parents either expected too much of their children at a particular age level so it was impossible to attain it, or the parents constantly changed the definition of the goal in the middle of the process so that, even if the children succeeded with the original goal, they still failed. Therefore, grown-up abused children are afraid to set goals because to do so is to ensure failure.

For all of these types of former victims, goal setting is a painful process. It is not something which has ever provided them with any meaningful satisfaction. If they were in the group that had little or no assistance with goal setting, they also had no experience of satisfaction because no one was available to give them feedback. They often did not know whether they had succeeded or failed because they received no response from their parents. No one cared whether they succeeded, no one was around to congratulate them and urge them on to greater successes.

Still another group of grown-up abused children learned that satisfactory goal attainment was impossible for them. No matter how successful or conscientious they were it was never good enough. No matter how high the grades they received in school, no matter how well they succeeded in sports or extracurricular activities, no matter how responsible they were about chores around the house, it was never good enough. They were still open to being ignored, ridiculed, or beaten. Over and over again, group members recount tales of how their accomplishments were turned into reasons for abuse. The achievement "wasn't good enough." They were "too arrogant" about their success. It was all "done for the wrong motives." The end result was that they never learned that it was possible for them to accomplish anything worthwhile. In fact, the inverse was true: they could never accomplish anything; they would never amount to anything.

The second group did not experience satisfaction because their goals were impossible to attain. They were simply too high or constantly changing. For the third set of former victims, no level of attainment could generate success. There was no way they could satisfy the expectations of their parents.

These latter two groups contain those who have experienced the most direct abuse related to goal setting. They were usually criticized, ridiculed, or physically abused for their failure to attain their parents' goals. These persons experience a definite fear of goal setting. They have had distinct negative associations with doing so. They *know* that goal setting has negative consequences and few, if any, positive results. For the first group, however, their problems arise more from an undefined anxiety and a simple lack of knowledge about the process to be followed.

Whatever the source of the problems with goal setting, this part of the group's process is extremely important. It is necessary for any group to function effectively, but for this clientele it has a practical therapeutic role. By practicing goal setting in the group, the members can learn to set reasonable and measurable goals for their lives so they can gain a sense of self-satisfaction and self-worth from their attainment.

The "reasonable and measurable" aspect of that last statement is also extremely difficult for former victims. Once the fear and anxiety are overcome (and that may have to be done repeatedly, each time new goals are established) much work must be done to ensure that the goals set are realistic and meaningful.

This problem, of course, stems from a lack of experience. With so little background to draw from, grown-up abused children have no effective measure of what is attainable. Some will set extremely high goals; others very low goals. Often this is a result of their lack of knowledge about what is realistic on either the high or the low end of the scale. Some, however, set their goals very high in an attempt to please the group leaders and as a way to get the praise and acceptance they never got as children. Others set their goals very low because of their low self-esteem and as an attempt to avoid failure.

The members of both groups must be worked with to find a realistic middle ground and then to break the goal attainment process down into manageable steps. All too often group members attempt to get from point A to point Z without realizing there may be 24 steps in between. Again this may often stem for their simple lack of experience; however, some of it also arises from their obsessive need to be perfect in order to finally get some approval. To take too long is a sign of weakness or imperfection and they will not get the acceptance they so desperately crave.

When members do set goals and begin to make changes and to grow, they frequently find themselves uneasy and uncomfortable with the changes. During this period their dependence on the group may increase, and they will credit any improvements in their condition to the group as a whole or to the leaders in particular. This too is a product of their abusive experience. They do not have enough self-esteem to give themselves any credit. This also is a defensive move; if they give the credit for achievements to the group or leader, they can also pass on the blame, if down the line, they should regress or fail.

Safety in Similarity

This same lack of self-esteem is also the basis on which members form relationships and alliances and it can prove counterproductive. Some members feel affinity for one another because of what they perceive as similar levels of coping.

Often we hear one member say to another, "I know just what you're feeling. I know what you're going through and that it is very difficult. You and I have a lot in common." This kind of statement is very reassuring and supportive for the one to whom it is spoken, and we encourage such empathetic responses between members.

However, sometimes this kind of response can be the beginning of a nonproductive alliance for either the supporter or the supportee, or both. Although such reassurance is essential if former victims are going to be freed of the sense of isolation and guilt which stem from their abusive experiences, it must not be allowed to become the basis for continuing inappropriate behaviors or as an excuse for not making necessary changes. It can happen that the participants in such an alliance are so relieved to find someone struggling with the same problem that the pressure for resolution is diminished. "If he (or she) has a similar difficulty, maybe it's okay to be this way."

The desire for safety in similarity often dictates this sense of identification and alliance. Both of the persons involved are familiar with their present patterns of behavior, and since they have now found someone else who identified with those same patterns, they can continue their present coping strategies without feeling isolated and bizarre.

Even if that dynamic does not influence the relationship between the two parties, another set of problems can arise when one of the persons begins to make changes. No matter which of the two people initiates a change in his or her life, the other person may feel betrayed and abandoned, and, in fact, may react negatively to the person who is changing. Accusations and put-downs are not uncommon as the abandoned partner acts out his or her frustration and even attempts to keep the other party at the same level of coping.

> On one occasion we had two people in the same group who were very quiet. Even though they did not say much to each other, there was an immediate affinity; they felt comfortable with one another. After participating in the group for several weeks and achieving a level of personal comfort with the group, Linda decided that one of her goals in the group was to become more assertive. She began to speak more freely and ask for time to share her concerns.
>
> As Linda became more and more active in the group her friend, Ellen, became even more quiet. Ellen's withdrawal became especially evident on occasions when Linda was talking about her concerns. On one occasion Linda shared that Ellen had snubbed her when they met one another outside the group.
>
> The group confronted Ellen and encouraged her to share what was troubling her. She began by attacking Linda, "You don't like me anymore. You never pay any attention to me. I used to feel close to you, but I don't anymore. I don't even know you anymore. I can't relate to you."

With the help of the group, Linda was able to respond positively to Ellen's charges. She pointed out that she was not rejecting Ellen and still felt a strong kinship with her but that she was also trying to accomplish one of her goals for joining the group. She hoped that Ellen would accept her as she continued to grow and that Ellen would also consider trying to be more assertive because Linda had found it a very positive experience.

Actually Ellen did begin to make her own changes, but she and Linda never reestablished their old, natural affinity. The stereotypes within which they had established their original relationship were no longer operational. Their association now had to be based on more realistic and complex data than the fact that they were both quiet.

Occasionally, such a stereotyping process takes place within the group as a whole. One member is perceived as the quiet one, another as the talker, still another as the vulnerable member who must be protected, and yet another as the strong member who "has it more together" and does not need the same care as the other members of the group. These roles are sometimes imposed by the other members of the group, but often are self-imposed by the former victims themselves. They learned these roles in their families, often as defense mechanisms, and continue to act them out in any group setting.

Therefore, it is important to confront stereotypes and rigid roles within the group so that members can learn new methods of behavior. Members can, in fact, learn that they need not try to blend into the background or control every situation by an incessant stream of words in order to be safe. They can experience being vulnerable without being belittled, or assertive without being attacked or ridiculed.

Specifically, we often ask people to try a new behavior for a meeting or series of meetings. For a certain meeting they will speak only after correctly repeating what another person has said. Someone will be told he or she will be expected to open the next session.

Members form alliances or define their role in the group based on their former family roles. Often in an abusive family, older siblings take the greater share of the abuse in order to protect the younger members of the family. Many times, the parenting role is thrust upon them when the adults in the family are unable or unwilling to do so. They tend to continue this role of parent and protector, coming to the rescue of anyone in the group who is being pressured, thus interfering with that person's growth process.

These self-appointed surrogate parents also fail to deal with their own problems. Since the primary and instinctive focus of their concern is on the other people in the group, they are unable to pay attention to their own needs. Although these group members are often very mature and personable and provide a great deal of assistance to the group leaders, they must be encouraged to deal with their own issues. It may be necessary to discuss their parenting propensities with them so they can consciously hold these in check while participating in a group where this role is not required of them and which is designed to free them of that responsibility. They must, in a sense, be taught to be concerned for their own growth and development.

We have already pointed out that the one consistent role in the family with which most abused children are familiar is that of the scapegoat. This too carries over into the group. Unconsciously, most of the members expect at some time to be the scapegoat. They are internally ready for it and they easily slip into behavior patterns which elicit such treatment. Heads bowed, they accept any critical feedback as a negative attack which they deserve. Subconsciously they may even wonder when the violence is going to begin.

To counteract this tendency the group leaders must continually point out the scapegoat tone which group members project for themselves: their aptness for putting themselves down, their eagerness to apologize and accept blame, their failure to hear words of support and praise or deal constructively with feedback offered to them.

The leaders must make sure members hear positive statements about themselves. They must even make members repeat the praise which has been offered them.

Feedback

The use of feedback is probably the most difficult ingredient of group process for a grown-up abused children's group to implement. This difficulty stems from three factors. As we just discussed above, grown-up abused children are accustomed to receiving primarily destructive and derogatory feedback. Therefore, they find it difficult to hear positive, laudatory feedback, even when it is offered.

If the feedback offered in the group is at all critical, recipients hear it as insulting and demeaning. No matter how positively and gently the feedback is phrased, the group members perceive a put-down and immediately become defensive. This is again consistent with their previous experience. All the feedback they received as children was negative and demeaning, a sign that someone did not like them. Therefore, it is now difficult for them to distinguish between criticism of their actions and criticism of themselves as people.

The final factor is that for former abuse victims, critical feedback did not stop at demeaning remarks, it often resulted in physical violence. They recall that such comments were frequently the prelude to violence. Therefore, that is their present expectation.

Given the last two factors, it is understandable that grown-up abused children's reaction to any form of feedback is fear. Any feedback is a potential source of physical or emotional pain, no matter what the source. Their first reaction is avoidance and self-preservation.

On the other hand, as the initiators of feedback they fear that if they begin communication related to anything negative, they might, like their parents, lose control and become abusive. They fear that they too might become destructive to others. This results in a minimum of feedback within the group and the use of many passive-aggressive forms of communication.

All of this, of course, greatly hampers the process of communication within the group. Group leaders must, therefore, spend a lot of time teaching and exemplifying feedback skills. They must explain the need for, importance of, and function of feedback within the life of the group.

The leaders must also clearly define the meaning and process of feedback. They must point out that it is possible to criticize specific behaviors of a person without attacking his or her personality. They must clarify the distinction between a person's behavior and its effect on observers of that behavior. All of this, of course, helps group members identify their own feelings about other people's behaviors and distinguish them from the behaviors themselves. All of the standard feedback techniques ("when you _____ I feel _____") must be taught and practiced in their simplest and most specific forms.

In short, feedback is going to happen in a grown-up abused children's group only if the leaders focus their attention on it as a process and teach the group members to do it. It is not going to happen naturally. Learning feedback skills must be a continuing process in the group.

CONCLUSION

The dynamics of abuse, therefore, have a continued impact upon the traditional intragroup roles of initiator, information giver, contributor, opinion giver, evaluator, and critic. Group members hesitate to accept any of the first four roles because a high level of visibility results and being too "visible" in their families led to abuse. The first four roles make them vulnerable to criticism—in their framework, attack—from others in the group. They see the role of evaluator and critic as the roles their parents had in their families and when that process began it ended in abuse. They resist assuming that role for themselves. They know how painful it can be on the receiving end of the process and they also do not trust themselves to be able to control what they say.

In conclusion, we have found that although grown-up abused children have many inherent difficulties functioning in a group setting, they also have a strong need and desire to be a part of a caring, supportive community. Their longing for understanding and acceptance moves them to overcome their inbred isolation and their fear of rejection. But even after they begin participating in a group, many of their preciously learned survival skills hinder their full sharing in the values of the group experience. Nonetheless, much of what the grown-up abused child needs to know and experience is available only through interactions in a group. Only in such a setting can they learn and practice social and communication skills so necessary for happy and productive lives.

The many evasive and manipulative tactics which former abuse victims developed (quite literally for survival) must be recognized as such, gently confronted, and carefully reformed so that the skill can still be used when appropriate but set aside when not needed. This makes it particularly important that sensitive and experienced group process facilitators lead the groups. The next chapter will consider their qualifications.

CHAPTER FOUR

THE GROUP LEADER

THE difficulties encountered in groups for grown-up abused children indicate the need for a group leader with special skills and a unique personality. All who have led such groups attest to the challenge and satisfaction they experience in working with such groups. However, they also admit to the great amount of energy, attention, and patience demanded of them.

Effective leaders are called upon to be understanding, patient, responsive to feelings, and comfortable with themselves and still be able to be appropriately firm counsellors and facilitators of group process. They must also act as role models for adults who have had few positive adult figures in their lives to emulate.

UNDERSTANDING

As one might expect, anyone working with a group of former abuse victims must have at least a basic understanding of the dynamics of family abuse. Leaders need not be experts on all the latest research on child abuse but they should have a working understanding of the interaction processes prevalent in abusive families. They need to appreciate how these processes tend to continue in later life and influence the former victims' adult relationships.

Blair and Rita Justice in their book, *The Abusive Family*, have identified "shifting symbiosis" as a major aspect of the abusing family's interaction process. By this they mean that the process of dependence between and among members of the family is constantly changing and is "not for cooperative mutual support and affection but for exploitation and the satisfaction of neurotic needs." (Justice & Justice, 1976, p. 70). In such a family it is not just the children who seek care and nurturance but the parents as well. There is a constant struggle to determine who can receive more care and have more of their needs satisfied. The responsibility for providing care shifts among all members of the family.

This struggle goes on without regard for age, maturity, role in the family, or level of ability to provide the care. Very simply, the loser in the battle ends up with the responsibility. Thus, when the child interferes with a parent's ability to get his or her needs met, or when the child fails to personally meet a parent's need, abuse occurs.

This continual struggle for nurturance and care creates constant change. Roles within the family are always being readjusted and reliable support systems are nonexistent. This is a major factor which contributes to the "comfort with chaos" we discussed in the last chapter.

Because of these shifting symbiotic relationships, normal dependency needs are never met and the family does not fulfill its task as a place where the children learn to meet their need to belong yet also learn to become individuals. The constant competition for caring in the abusive family is so dysfunctional that children do not learn to differentiate themselves as individuals. They cannot feel strong and independent or comfortable with themselves. They do not believe they can care for themselves and they believe that in order to survive they must find someone who will take care of them. The search for nurturance moves outside the family. The process of manipulating others to meet their needs finds new targets and what Ray Helfer (1978, pp. 33-77) in his book, *Childhood Comes First*, calls the World of Abnormal Rearing (W.A.R.) expands into new arenas and inappropriate areas of their lives such as their workplace, their friendships, or their new families.

This World of Abnormal Rearing continues to influence other aspects of the victims' lives. Grown-up abused children carry with them dysfunctional methods for getting their needs met, guilt for not fulfilling unrealistic expectations, and confusion over their roles and responsibilities. As Helfer so aptly describes it, these former victims are so caught in a tight circle, bounded by feelings of "I'm no good," "I can't trust anyone," and "I don't deserve anything good" that they do not know how to relate to anyone in a positive manner. These factors contribute to the symptoms noted in Chapter One, and the group leaders must recognize that they form the context within which group members have learned to relate to others. This must be fully appreciated if the leaders are going to be able to help the group members break out of this destructive circle; if they are to help them learn to appreciate themselves, trust others, and recognize that they have legitimate needs and every right in the world to have them met.

This intellectual understanding and appreciation should not, however, be translated too quickly into an emotional understanding. One of the easiest ways to earn the scorn and distrust of group members is to claim, "I know just how you feel. I know what it's like." This can bring sudden and sometimes vicious reactions: "No, you don't and you never will. This has never happened to you and you can never know what it's like." Such responses are clearly justified. All the intellectual knowledge in the world cannot give a nonvictim a true understanding of the depth of pain and fear.

Former victims do not want superficial sympathy; they want an attentive and sympathetic hearing of their situation. They want to be heard and believed without horror or disgust and without judgment or condemnation. Once their situation is understood and appreciated, they can move to solutions and resolution of the feelings they have.

In order to facilitate this process the group leaders must also understand the progression of growth and change which grown-up abused children experience when resolving the effects of their abuse. There does, in fact, seem to be a common process which grown-up abused children need to go through in order to resolve the effects of their abusive childhood. This process is fairly consistent but it does not flow smoothly in one direction. There are frequent new beginnings as different aspects of their abuse experience are identified and confronted.

The first step is that former victims actually acknowledge the fact of their abuse. This is not as simple as it may seem. Sometimes victims do not remember certain aspects of their abuse, e.g. they remember physical beatings but not sexual assaults. Even when they do remember the violence, they must also be able to label it as abuse. They must acknowledge that the beatings they received were not typical and acceptable methods of parental discipline. What happened to them was excessive and inappropriate and it was something for which they were not to blame. They must be able to distinguish their responsibility from that of their parents.

Naturally, this step must have begun before a person even enters a group. At least, they must have identified themselves as victims of child abuse, even if they are not conscious of all the facets of their experience. The former victims must also have determined who was responsible for the abuse before they enter a group. They must have moved beyond the need to attribute blame for what happened to the process of learning to cope with the effects of their experience.

> One of the few times we have had to ask a person to leave a group was a woman, Jean, whose only concern was trying to understand why her parents did what they did and why other family members, neighbors, and even the authorities, when they did get involved, did not make more of an effort to stop the abuse. Despite the fact that the group offered a wide variety of possible explanations: your parents did not know any better or they were sick; your neighbors were afraid to get involved; the authorities did not have enough evidence or enough legal power, Jean was never satisfied. The same questions kept coming back. We finally pointed out that without extensive interviews with the various people involved, it was impossible to answer her questions and that what was more important was that she deal with the results of the abuse. Although no one could do anything about the past and peoples' lack of involvement, something could be done about the present.
>
> Whenever the topic shifted to her own present condition or to the concerns of other members of the group, Jean would simply tune out. After several attempts to deal with this behavior, it was decided, in consultation with her therapist, that Jean would no longer participate in the group. Her therapist was to call us when she felt that Jean was able to participate effectively in a group process. That call has not come yet.

Once that principally intellectual process of recognizing and acknowledging the nature of their abuse has been accomplished, the grown-up abused children must move to the next step in the process: identifying and resolving their emotional response to those experiences. This, too, is not as simple as it may seem. It raises many conflicting emotions.

In most cases the persons responsible for their abuse were people close to them and the very persons society has told them they are to love and respect. The former victim also wants desperately to feel genuine affection for those persons who abused them or failed to protect them. Their hope of someday achieving a loving, intimate relationship with their parents has often been their only source of consolation. To fully acknowledge their anger and disappointment would, they fear, destroy their last vestige of hope for a "real" family relationship. It would be the end of their chances for a normal family experience. Therefore, grown-up abused children provide numerous rationalizations for their parents' behavior, and they block and deny their own emotional reactions to what happened to them.

Besides this continuing hope for a normal family life, grown-up abused children also find this step in the process difficult because it involves acknowledging and expressing intense feelings of anger and resentment. In other parts of this book, we have discussed, at great length, the problems and fears related to this as well as methods for achieving resolution.

The next step in the process, and again a more intellectual one, is that the former victims must recognize the continuing impact their abusive pasts have on their present behavior. This means that they must realize how that past experience colors their perceptions of and responses to people and situations in their present. They need to learn to recognize when their present responses are inappropriate. Their inappropriate responses may range from inordinate fear of anyone in authority to mistrust of everyone they meet, from fear of success to excessive striving for perfection, from insecurity in social situations to problems with sexuality. The possible situations are numerous and varied.

As part of this step, the grown-up abused children need to learn to distinguish between situations in their past and similar experiences in the present. They must learn to differentiate people who have authority over them in the present from abusive persons in their past. They must begin to recognize and control the transferences they may be making between their past and their present.

The final step in the process is for grown-up abused children to learn and apply alternate methods of performing tasks, relating to people, and responding to situations. This step grows naturally but slowly out of the previous steps. Once the inappropriateness of previous methods are acknowledged, the former victims can explore new options, choose new procedures, and practice applying them in various situations. However, they are only free to do this after they have recognized and resolved some of the previously discussed influences of their abusive experience. Only by confronting the various intellectual and emotional components of their abusive past are grown-up abused children able to achieve control over their emotional and behavioral responses to the present.

As we said at the beginning of this section, these steps are consistent but do not always flow continually in one direction. As new issues arise and as the former victims confront different aspects of their experiences, the process must be started again and the sources of present problems traced to the previous experiences which are influencing the present feelings and behaviors. The important thing is that the leaders know where the group member is in the process so they can provide the most helpful guidance.

PATIENT

For this guidance to be truly helpful, the group leaders must also develop a tremendous amount of patience as a product of the understanding and appreciation they have gained. The dysfunction engendered by abnormal rearing is longstanding, and the destructive relationship patterns are deeply embedded. In turn, the process of change will also be time consuming and painful.

Leaders must be prepared to accept and work with deeply ingrained behavior patterns which, though objectively self-destructive, were the only ones the victims learned and the only ones which functioned well in their "abnormal world." Victims do not easily recognize such patterns as "wrong" or inappropriate in the context of the world outside their abusive home nor can they easily change them once they recognize the need to do so.

Many paralyzing fears and nonrational behaviors arise for former victims as a result of their abnormal rearing. Tasks and activities which persons from more "normal" childhoods might find relatively simple and nonthreatening create major traumas for grown-up abused children. For example, the prospect of meeting new people can induce feelings of terror; the need to express their feelings, fears, or hopes or the task of making a decision can immobilize them and make them literally unable to talk; even the experience of success or praise can create major discomfort and anxiety for them. The leader must be able to appreciate the degree of difficulty involved in certain tasks and must be able to offer sympathetic reinforcement and support.

One male group member exhibited particular difficulty carrying out normal activities.

> Ed was first referred to a grown-up abused children group by a concerned faculty member. Although he was an exceptionally bright student, Ed was unable to complete the most basic class work and was extremely unsure of himself in any setting, in or out of the classroom.
>
> When he first began to attend the group, Ed appeared completely frightened, kept his eyes cast down, and avoided contact with others both before and after meetings. Although he attended regularly, he participated only minimally in the group. He would respond "Yes" and "No" to questions, but when any question demanded a more extensive response he would ask to be excused from answering.
>
> The group members were very patient with Ed. They were always willing to let him maintain his silence, and they made supportive statements: that they were pleased that he continued to come, and that they hoped that he would soon be able to share further with them. In response to this Ed would simply nod appreciatively. If the group leaders attempted to pressure Ed to take a more active role, the other members would come to his rescue, supporting his right to maintain his silence.
>
> This went on for some months; gradually Ed's responses became a bit more complete, his answers grew to more than one syllable. The story which slowly emerged revealed severe violence and neglect in his infancy which included long hours locked in a dark closet, much ridicule, and brutal beatings. Despite having several older brothers and sisters, he did not learn to speak until he was four years old.
>
> The isolation, fear, and lack of opportunity to communicate in his childhood carried over into his school years. Although Ed had a near-genius IQ, he was unable to relate to and communicate with his teachers, and he did poorly in school. Nevertheless, working primarily on his own, he had been able to master many complicated aspects of physics and math, even though he was always too frightened and insecure to share what he knew with his teachers.
>
> After many months of regular attendance and progressively increasing participation in the group, Ed was able to share some of his ideas and mathematical formulas with group members. Most of them confessed complete inability to understand Ed's formulas, but this too proved to be a learning experience for him. He realized that people's failure to understand or to respond with enthusiasm did not mean rejection.
>
> Ed continued to attend the group for several months and increased his participation. Still, there were many false starts and many sullen silences. It took much support and cajoling by both the leaders and the group members to keep the communicating moving. After a time Ed began to share his ideas with people outside the group, but he always came back to

the group for support. "I am going to talk with Professor _____. . . Does this sound like a good way to approach it? . . . I need some encouragement."

To this day, Ed continues to need periodic strong doses of encouragement. He has, however, overcome much of the fear and distrust which contributed to his continual academic failure.

The level of distrust engendered in most abused children also means that the leaders must be prepared to accept a tremendous amount of "testing." Often it will seem that the former victim wants to be rejected, wants the relationship to fail. Numerous trials will be imposed on the group leaders as the members try to determine the points on which the leaders cannot be trusted. Members are always subconsciously asking, "When will they become angry and maybe even abusive? . . . What will make them dislike me and reject me? . . . When will they recognize what a terrible person I am? . . . How long will they put up with me before they give up and tell me how dumb, hopeless, and impossible to work with I really am?" Sometimes these questions are asked explicitly and repeatedly: "Do you still like me?" Other times they are silently attached to other statements: "Look at what a mess I have made of my life"; "No, I wasn't able to accomplish that (simple) task again." But whatever the form of the tests, the results are carefully tabulated. No matter what the method of inquiry, the leader must be prepared to answer patiently with constant reinforcement and reassurance. The reassurance must be explicit and strong because it must penetrate the screen of a predetermined sense of rejection.

Inherent in this testing is the process of transference. As one might expect, grown-up abused children have a lot of residual fear, dislike, and anger toward their abusive parent. These feelings frequently get directed toward whichever group leader most nearly resembles that parent. Therefore, the forms of testing administered to leaders vary greatly depending on the sex of the leader. Also, the degree of a leader's acceptance or rejection by a group member varies according to the same factor. This is a major reason why we insist on a male and female leader for each group. There must be opportunity for the different transferences to be resolved.

It is easy to understand and even expected that the leader who is the same sex as the abusive parent will receive negative transference and testing. However, testing will not be limited to that leader. As much, if not more, testing and hostility will be directed at the leader representing the nonabusive parent. Victims feel a great deal of anger and distrust toward the parent who did not protect them. Generally, this anger is not as conscious or clearly defined as the anger toward the abusive parent. Therefore, the leaders will have to allot a great amount of time, patience, and careful analysis to helping the group members understand and acknowledge this aspect of their anger.

This problem becomes even more difficult if the nonabusive parent was also victimized. In such a case, that parent may be idealized. Even though he or she did not protect the child, the parent is seen as a fellow victim and even a martyr. That ideal image is then transferred to the same-sex leader, with the result that this leader can do or say nothing wrong and the other nothing right.

In one such group situation we tried to use this transference process to our advantage.

> Roger had been the victim of an especially violent father. Beatings had been frequent and brutal, occasionally resulting in the need for medical treatment. Although Roger had most often been the victim of the attacks, his mother had also been beaten. She apparently took the beatings passively and without complaining.
>
> When Roger would talk about his father, he himself would become violent, stamping his feet, pounding the arms of his chair and cursing loudly. However, any mention of his mother would immediately calm him. He would talk softly and gently about what a dear, sweet woman she was and how she had been "a living saint to put up with that bastard." Any attempt to discuss why she had stayed in the relationship and allowed the beatings of both of them to go on was dismissed: "She couldn't help it. He was too big."
>
> From his very first meeting Roger was drawn to the female leader of the group. He was attentive to anything she said or did, complimenting her on her appearance as well as on any comments she made. Whenever possible he would sit next to her. None of the other women received similar attention. At the end of each meeting Roger would thank the leader profusely for her help and support. Usually these comments were accompanied by remarks about how much she reminded him of his mother.
>
> On the other hand, his reaction to the male leader was exactly the opposite. He would sit as far away from him as possible and turn his chair away. He dismissed the male leader's comments, and no matter what had transpired during the meeting, Roger usually concluded the session by saying he did not think the male leader liked him.
>
> After this had gone on for several weeks, with Roger making very little progress in dealing with his own problems, the leaders decided to try the

"good guy, bad guy" team approach. The female leader took on the "bad guy" role with the responsibility of offering critical feedback and pressuring Roger for more change and response. The male leader, already cast in the "bad guy" role, was to take on the task of being the sensitive, sympathetic and supportive "good guy." No matter what the need for criticism or pressure, the male leader was to leave all of that to the female and simply compliment and praise Roger for whatever he had done well.

This plan was carried out for some weeks but Roger's responses did not change. No matter how critical, pushy, and in her words, "bitchy" the female leader was to Roger in any session, she was still thanked and praised profusely. And, of course, the male leader was attacked for his lack of sensitivity. Finally, even the other group members were noting and pointing out Roger's misperceptions. People were coming to the defense of the male group leader. Roger was finally forced to make some distinctions between his father and other men in authority and between his mother and other women in authority. He at least toned down his respective praise and criticism, his more explicit forms of transference. However, in the remaining weeks until the group disbanded for the summer Roger never really changed his nonverbal responses to the two leaders.

This orchestration procedure, although only mildly successful, was one attempt to use the transference process as a means of therapy for a group member. Transference is certain to occur. The leaders must be prepared for and must patiently work through this long and complicated process.

Other personality processes learned in an abusive family, which require great patience on the part of the leaders, are evasion and manipulation. These processes usually have negative connotations in our culture. Manipulative and evasive people are thought to be up to no good, trying to get something they do not deserve or to get out of something they do deserve. For grown-up abused children, however, these are basic and essential survival skills. These are the methods they learned in order to avoid the abuse they did not deserve, and to get the attention and caring which should have been theirs automatically.

The problem is that these skills are now almost instinctive for former victims. They use them without thinking. They apply them to situations in which they are no longer necessary or appropriate. As we discussed in Chapter Three, these methods may even be counterproductive for what the former victim really wants to accomplish. These procedures often distort very important messages which the grown-up abused child wants to convey.

In the efforts to change these deeply ingrained instincts, leaders must be ready to provide careful and patient analysis of present behavior, to point out the ineffectiveness of that behavior in most present situations, and to help members develop and practice new forms of behavior. Since deeply ingrained and previously vital instincts are being challenged, they will not be quickly or easily reformed.

RESPONSIVE TO FEELINGS

Grown-up abused children quite naturally have many emotions related to their abusive experience. Unfortunately, they are not in touch with their feelings. (Both of these seemingly contradictory statements are true.) The emotions are deep and pervade all aspects of their life, but they are ill-defined and often associated with extreme guilt. These emotions are strong, but they are improperly directed.

As we pointed out in Chapter Two on group goals, one of the major tasks of a grown-up abused children's group is to help the members get in touch with their own feelings. The leaders must make this clear at the outset by emphasizing that the expression of emotions is expected and that such revelations will be supported and encouraged. They need to indicate that no emotion is taboo, that all emotions will be respected, and that the group will spend time discussing them, focusing them, and finding appropriate and effective ways to express them.

This simple statement will not, however, immediately unleash pent-up emotions. Because the families of group members discouraged and even punished the expression of any feelings, this is a difficult process to initiate. Too many messages to the contrary have been internalized over the years. Even if group members can identify feelings, they often do not know any appropriate ways to express them. Over and over again feelings must be probed in the context of present incidents in the group and memories of specific incidents in their homes. This will begin with intellectual discussions about what feelings might have been appropriate then and which ones might still be fitting, as well as discussions about what feelings are proper and how they might be expressed.

Often, however, all feelings are denied, despite the contradicting messages of body language and inappropriate affect. In these cases, the leaders need to gently point out that certain feelings would surely be natural in this situation and that such feelings are acceptable. This demands that the leaders themselves be clear about the possible range of emotions appropriate to specific negative events. They must also be able to identify and discuss with group members the kinds of feelings which might be associated with such events. They should even be able to describe in physical terms what various emotions might be like.

Many former abuse victims have so effectively blocked feelings out of their lives that they do not even know they are having them. Often leaders have to ask, "Do you feel tenseness in your shoulders? Or knots in your stomach? Do you get headaches? Do you find yourself clenching your fists until they hurt?" Once such physiological reactions have been identified (and most group members feel freer to admit such reactions than to admit to certain emotions which have value connotations), then their meaning and their possible relationship to specific emotions can be discussed. This frees the group member to consider different possible emotions for a specific event, i.e. fear, hurt, anger, and become progressively comfortable with identifying a specific one.

As possible emotions are considered, the group leader can be helpful by pointing out their legitimacy and noting that there is a wide range of acceptable and unacceptable methods for expressing each emotion. In this way the negative connotations of certain emotions (i.e., anger always hurts someone) can be minimized.

Sometimes group members will not act on feelings they have within the group and will try to mask them. Therefore, it is important for the leaders to be constantly aware of how all the members might be feeling. This is another reason why it is important to have two group leaders. If a particular member or group of members are actively involved in a discussion or are experiencing some crisis, one of the leaders can pay attention to that event while the other observes the rest of the group.

Even if members are not actively involved in the discussion, they may nonetheless be having strong reactions. The issue may be eliciting powerful emotions or triggering recollections and flashbacks from their past. The second leader can observe all the members of the group in order to note what else is happening and to focus the attention of the group on these other reactions when the time is appropriate. Two specific examples will help illustrate this point.

Carla had been an active and articulate member of the group for some months. Her comments and responses to others were always appropriate and helpful. However, the leaders began to notice a pattern. Whenever anything happened in the group which involved anger, Carla withdrew. If people were discussing their feelings about anger, she became quiet. If people were actually expressing their anger at someone in the group or at their absent parents, she would physically push her chair back and grip the arms of the chair tightly.

With a second leader available to respond to these cues, we were able to confront Carla with her behavior and gradually get her to discuss her reactions to anger. Initially, the discussions focused on her fear that any anger was ultimately going to be directed at her; therefore, her shrinking back was self defense.

Gradually it became clear that Carla was also afraid of her own anger. Often the anger expressed in the group resonated with her own feelings. She wanted to voice her own feelings; she wanted to lash out with her long-repressed hostility. However, she was afraid of what she would do with that anger. She was afraid that even if she merely voiced it she would lose control and begin to strike out. She was certain she would never be able to stop. Her white-knuckled grasp on the chair was to keep her from lashing out. After much discussion and applying some of the physical expression methods discussed in Chapter Two, Carla soon learned to handle her feelings of anger and to contribute to group discussions about this topic.

Because of the nature of discussions about and expressions of anger in a grown-up abused children's group, it would have been difficult for one leader to have properly responded to Carla's anxiety. It might have gone completely unnoticed.

On another occasion two women members of the group got into a very heated exchange. The discussion was fast and furious between the two of them. It took the full attention of one of the leaders to make sure they were hearing one another and responding accurately.

During the exchange one of the male members of the group, Henry, tried to contribute to this discussion. Henry is normally soft-spoken and there was no way a soft-spoken comment was going to be heard in the midst of this active exchange. Soon he became discouraged and withdrew from the whole process. He lit a cigarette and gazed out the window.

When the discussion finally concluded, the second group leader was able to ask Henry what he had been trying to say. He denied that he had tried to intervene and that he had anything at all to say. After some minutes of discussion Henry finally admitted that he had tried to say something, but now he was too angry about being ignored to even want to participate. The people in the group were just like his family, he said; they ignored him and didn't think anything he had to say was important. If that was the way the group was going to treat him, he had "nothing more to say."

After extensive group discussion of the process of the previous discussion and of Henry's overly soft-spoken manner, and after some apologies from the two women, Henry was finally able to make his comments. He also came to see that what had happened was not a rejection of him, that he needed to understand and accept group processes better, and that he also needed to assert himself more.

Henry's passive method of responding to his anger and frustration made it virtually impossible for a single leader to identify his need. He never would have had an opportunity to express his feelings unless a second leader had been available to identify his frustration.

Appropriate expression is not only a problem with the difficult and painful emotions. As we pointed out in Chapter One, even positive emotions such as joy or satisfaction were often punished in abusive families. The exuberance of a joyful child was considered disruptive and annoying. Treated as a negative action, it was often severely punished. The message communicated was "You should not be happy." If children in an abusive family were successful at some activity and shared with their parents their satisfaction at a job well done, they were often ridiculed for thinking it was something important or punished for being proud and boastful. The message was: "What you do is not good enough, and it is wrong to feel good about yourself and your accomplishments." The ultimate message: "Do not allow emotions into your life. They will only be the source of trouble and pain."

Given this childhood context, it is easy to understand why former victims have trouble allowing themselves to have positive feelings as adults. They are reluctant to share their accomplishments with others, afraid to allow themselves to be happy. Therefore, it is important for the group leaders to program into the meetings some time when the members can share some of the good things that happen to them. They must make sure that the sessions do not simply become heavy and depressing problem sessions. Sometimes we have begun sessions by asking members to share one good thing that has happened to them during the week or to share one accomplishment from the past week of which they are proud. For many this is extremely difficult, and they have to be prodded and assisted. Specific possibilities need to be suggested. "What about that project you were working on?" "What about the term paper you were writing?" "Weren't you helping your neighbor with his garden? How did that go?"

When members share their accomplishments, the leaders must respond honestly and enthusiastically. They must show true appreciation for what has been done and let the group member know when success is recognized. They should elicit responses from the other members so that the member who is sharing can feel the full extent of that recognition. This process also enables all members to experience the feelings associated with giving praise. Such acts of positive reinforcement were not common in their families.

The group leader also must not let the group members negate their own accomplishments. Too often, even after someone's success has been acknowledged by group members, that person will be the first to denigrate it with an: "It was easy." or "I was lucky." Leaders must confront such remarks and reinforce the true value of the accomplishments. It should be made clear that there is no need to negate or deny what one has accomplished. The legitimate pride and joy of satisfaction should be encouraged and supported.

For one group member this provided an especially moving experience.

> Kathy was a closet artist. She talked often about "my art," but few people had seen any of it. Frequently members of the group asked to see her work, but Kathy would always "forget" to bring any along. Even when the group leaders assured her that it would definitely be appropriate for her to bring her works to the group, she resisted doing so. Finally one of the group members bribed Kathy by promising to perform a task which was difficult for him if Kathy would bring in some of her work.
>
> The following week Kathy arrived with a small packet among her books. She quickly put everything behind her chair. Early in the meeting Kathy was asked about her art. Immediately she asked, "Do you really want to see this? Are you sure it's all right to do this during the meeting?" When she could not delay the inevitable any longer, she produced the work.
>
> The group members took a real interest in the work. Each one spent considerable time with several of the pieces. They asked how certain techniques were performed and how certain effects were achieved. Kathy answered all the questions with a tone of amazement in her voice. When everyone was finished and the works had been returned to their packet, Kathy was asked how she felt. After a long silence she said, "I don't know

what to say. You people actually looked at them. You took a long time with them. You seemed to be really interested. Nobody's ever done that before. This feels really good." The group sat quietly for some time while Kathy silently experienced the glow of an accomplishment acknowledged.

On the other hand, supposedly negative emotions such as anger raise a distinct set of problems. As we noted in Chapter One, anger, as abused children have seen it expressed, is destructive and abusive. They do not want to repeat what they have seen. Also, if the anger they are experiencing is directed toward their parents, they feel guilty for having such feelings toward those for whom they are supposed to feel love. Furthermore, they fear that if they start to express their anger, they will never be able to stop. They fear that the years of repressed anger will consume their lives and they will be constantly angry at everything and everyone.

It has been our experience that this can be a critical point for many group members. Once a member has acknowledged anger and its legitimacy (we have noted that many actually begin by denying that they have ever felt angry) and has confronted the fear attached to that feeling, then he or she needs to find appropriate ways to express it.

The assistance of the group leaders can be critical at this point. Because they recognize the legitimacy and need for expression of these emotions they can provide needed support. They can also suggest and help the group member determine appropriate forms of expression.

Sometimes a thorough but calm discussion of past events and the feelings associated with them is enough. However, more often, such a discussion will cease to be calm. The former victim will break down in tears or break out in angry curses, or both. The group leaders need to be understanding, supportive, and even encouraging, assuring the member that such responses are necessary and good. The leaders may even suggest a few of their own favorite curse words for the occasion.

In Chapter Two we discussed at length the need some former victims have to express their pent-up anger physically. It will usually be up to the group leaders to suggest this as a possibility. It should not be forced upon the group member, but it can be offered as an option. Specific suggestions can be made: throwing pillows and punching overstuffed chairs in the meeting room, setting up a punching bag at home.

Leaders should point out to the group member that at first he or she should practice expressing such emotions only in a controlled environment such as the group. In this setting people are present who can provide an assurance of control in the situation. They are available to help the person regain control, should that be necessary. They can insure that the member does not hurt him or herself or anyone or anything else. Also there are people present who can provide encouragement and support while the anger episode is going on and with whom the experience can be processed and analyzed after it is over.

Group members will need to be reassured that this will not be a continuing and constant part of their life; that a few anger episodes will help them put the emotion into its proper perspective in their lives and enable them to get on with their lives with a new sense of relief and freedom. Although they will continue to experience anger about their past and will find plenty of opportunities to be angry in the future, other more commonly accepted forms of expression, such as a long run or a vigorous game of squash, will serve to express and dissipate the feeling.

In the controlled and supportive environment of the group, members are free to let the full range of their emotions run their course. They can allow their fantasies to run the gamut. And, most important, they can learn that they are able to gain control over their emotions and fantasies. The sense of awareness and control which they gain over their emotional life provides them with a great sense of freedom and self-confidence. They are now able to allow a wide range of long-repressed feelings into their lives: the good and enjoyable as well as the bad and the painful.

COMFORTABLE WITH THEMSELVES

In order to be supportive of this kind of process it is clear that the group leaders must be comfortable with their own emotions and with allowing others to express theirs. They must be able to allow emotional expression to run its full course and not cut it off prematurely. They must, therefore, be clear with themselves about how they feel about various emotions, anger in particular. Is it all right to feel angry? Is it all right to express anger? What forms and methods of expression are acceptable? The leaders must be clear about what they can accept and support in these areas.

This clarity is also important if leaders are to be sensitive enough to support those in the group who may be frightened by expressions of anger. Most group members will react to someone else's anger with fear. They are immediately convinced that they are at fault and that they are the object of the anger. They expect to be physically attacked, since this has been their previous experience. So they need frequent reassurance and comfort. The leaders must point out the real reasons for the anger and must emphasize that the members are not a part of those reasons.

Even though members become anxious when anger is expressed in the group, this experience can be helpful to all members. In this setting they will be able to see, possibly for the first time in their lives, that anger can be expressed without anyone being hurt. They can learn that anger is a normal and healthy reaction to certain situations and that it can have positive results.

The group leaders must also be clear about their own emotions. There will be times in the group when the slow pace of members' development, the manipulative and evasive tactics, and the frequent testing will put a severe strain on the leaders' frustration tolerance. Because former victims possess a high level of sensitivity, they will quickly note any frustration, exasperation, or anger. Most often, the group members will not raise the issue and confront it, but will simply internalize the leaders' frustration as another message about how bad they, the members, are. The group leaders must, therefore, be sensitive to their own feelings and be quick to acknowledge them to the group. Then the feelings and their causes can be discussed. The leaders can then make the necessary distinction between being upset with a person's behavior and continuing to accept the person, and the group can deal with the sources of the anger or frustration.

Every experienced group leader realizes that not all the frustration which he or she may feel during a group meeting originates in the group. Pressures and tensions of everyday life overflow into the group even for the most experienced group leader. These feelings are also perceived by the group members but they will believe that they are the cause of them. Therefore, it is also necessary to acknowledge such concerns to the group: "My kids have been a pain this week"; "My job is driving me crazy"; "My husband and I had an argument last night." This not only serves to clear the air and point out to the group members that they are not at fault; it also provides some important role models for the group members to follow.

Such sharing by leaders has often been the starting point for fruitful discussions. Group members are amazed that persons whom they respect and consider to be "normal" can have "negative" feelings and experiences. They are amazed to learn that disagreements and even anger happen in "normal" families and can be resolved without violence. Of course, none of these discussions can take place unless the group leaders are aware of their feelings and are willing to share them with the group.

Another emotion which grown-up abused chldren frequently need to express is sorrow. They have repressed much disappointment and anguish over the years. The group leaders must be prepared to support members in their pain. Doing this effectively may involve touching and physical contact.

Many former victims have a great need for someone who can comfort them in their sorrow. Until now most of their tears have been solitary ones. Although they cannot consciously ask for it, many of them hunger for some form of soothing contact: a hand to clasp, an arm around the shoulder, a warm embrace. Leaders must be able to read the nonverbal cues to know when to initiate such contact. They must also be able to read past the verbal messages which say "Don't touch me," to the repressed desire for physical warmth and contact. For many formerly abused children, physical contact was a painful experience. They cannot believe that it can be soothing and comforting, even though they desperately want it to be so.

Once again, the group leaders must be comfortable enough with themselves to be able to respond to the needs of group members for physical warmth, and to offer a reassuring hand clasp and a comforting embrace. Actually the group is the most helpful place for such contact to take place. Members' fears of possible sexual overtones and connotations are minimized by the presence of other people and the embarrassment for feeling such a need can be assuaged by the reassurances of other group members. This was rather comically illustrated on one occasion:

> Barbara came to one meeting with a Xeroxed page from a magazine

clutched in her hand. She played with it furtively throughout most of the meeting. Finally she said, "I have something I would like to share with the group. I found this article in a magazine." She then proceeded to read a short article which claimed that people need six hugs per day to maintain good mental health.

Sheepishly Barbara asked, "Could I ask if people here would give me a hug? I really feel a need for that." The group response was overwhelming, "Of course, but only if we can all get one in return."

From that day forward every session ended with a "group hug." Everyone got their chance to hug every other member of the group.

This incident has been reported to other groups and every one has incorporated the "group hug" into their closing ritual. Group members have also reported that they have occasionally greeted one another in this manner on campus or on the street. The group leaders have sometimes been greeted with, "I'm having a hard day. Can I have a hug?" Such requests are never refused.

Another area where the group leaders must also be clear about their own feelings is concerning the issue of abuse itself. They must be able to react with sensitivity to the accounts of abuse which they are going to hear, but not overreact. Expressions of horror or disbelief are not helpful to the former victims. They already know how horrible it was. They do not have to be reminded and they do not want their accounts to be the source of distress for the very persons who are supposed to be helping them.

On the other hand, the leaders must make it clear to the group members that they understand the nature of the abuse which occurred and that they accept and appreciate the anger and hostility the former victims may be expressing. This is necessary if any level of trust is going to be established. Many group members who have sought private counselling regarding their abuse have had negative experiences. Counselors have rejected or ridiculed their accounts or they have dismissed the connection between the past abuse and present problems. Too often the former victim has been told, "That happened fifteen years ago; it has nothing to do with your problem now. Forget about it." The leaders must therefore sometimes fight an uphill battle to earn the trust of group members.

Most leaders will experience a lot of anger toward the parents of the people with whom they are working. Such anger is appropriate and should be expressed, but in such a way that it does not demand a similar reaction from the former abused child. He or she may not yet be ready to deal with that long-repressed anger. Seeing that someone else is angry about what happened can be a freeing experience, but instant liberation or agreement should not be expected.

Furthermore, many grown-up abused children need and want to maintain a relationship with their parents. No matter what their parents did to them, they are still their parents and that bond needs to be preserved. Overly negative and condemnatory remarks about their parents can make members feel they should hate them and sever all relationships. Even if this were physically possible, it might well destroy their last sense of contact with a family, no matter how poor that might have been.

Frequently, members need to maintain this contact at a distance: making separate living arrangements, visiting only infrequently and under carefully controlled circumstances, and preparing themselves emotionally beforehand. While such visits may seem contrived or forced to an outsider, it may well be the only type of family contact the abuse victim can deal with comfortably. Thus, it needs to be maintained.

On at least one occasion a member's need to maintain a semblance of family life caused an unusual form of stress for one group leader:

> Denise participated in a group for a full school year. Her accounts of extreme physical and sexual abuse involving both of her parents were shared only with great difficulty. However, with the help of the group as well as a private therapist she was able to resolve many of her personal and sexual identity questions. When the group reconvened for the next school year, she decided that she did not need to participate.
> Late in that second year, there was a special dinner on campus to which parents were invited. Halfway through the evening Denise approached one of the leaders who was attending the dinner. She had brought her parents and she wanted him to meet them. She introduced him as the campus minister with whom she had worked on many projects. Her parents were very well dressed, both in tailored suits. They and the leader had a pleasant conversation for several minutes about their respective professions and their involvement in local church projects. They exchanged long lists of names of clergy with whom they had all worked at one time or another. The conversation ended cordially with warm handshakes all around.
> This incident lasted only fifteen minutes but the cognitive dissonance made it seem like hours. This leader was meeting and conversing with a set of parents who were evidently successful professionals, active church

members, and respected participants in their community; yet he was aware that they had also performed some of the worst forms of child abuse he had ever heard. The internal disparity was tremendous.

The leader gained a new appreciation of why Denise had had difficulty getting assistance from her pastor and her school counselors when she had approached them as a teenager. Her parents fit none of the stereotypes associated with child abuse. Her accusations had been dismissed as the rantings of a confused adolescent. The leader might have been similarly inclined had he not been aware of the anguish and pain involved in Denise's earlier disclosures.

The question has sometimes been raised whether former abuse victims themselves can be group leaders or whether all leaders should be former victims. This is a complex issue. One woman who contacted us about joining a group changed her mind because the leaders were not former victims. She did not believe nonvictims could adequately understand or treat victims. In actual fact, at times former victims have served as leaders of groups in our program, but this experience has had both positive and negative aspects.

Despite the one woman's insistence that a nonvictim could not help her, those leaders who were victims have reported that at least initially some of the group members tended to look more to the other (nonvictim) leader for guidance and support. (This perception was confirmed by the nonvictim leader.) It seemed as if another former victim, even though a leader of the group, could not provide the same insight and guidance as someone who had had "normal" childhood experiences. The initial assumption seemed to be: "If you had the same experiences as I did, you must be as 'bad' as I am and have the same problems I do. Therefore, I can't value your advice as highly as the other leader's."

However, those reporting also pointed out that this distinction between leaders diminished quickly and that group members soon came to respect and value the guidance and support of both equally. Nonetheless, the initial response had to be taken into consideration.

On the other hand, there is a certain validity to the woman's desire to have a former victim as a group leader. Nonvictims cannot fully understand or appreciate the experiences that victims have had and the difficulties they continue to face. A nonvictim can learn to understand intellectually what an abuse victim has experienced, but can never fully appreciate the terror and anguish, the shame and guilt, and the profound sense of self-deprecation that abuse can engender.

Again and again group members have responded angrily to our prodding and pressure for change: "You don't know how it feels!"; "You don't know how difficult this is to do!" Our answer has simply been, "You're right. I don't know. I know how I feel when you tell me about it, but I have never experienced it myself. I can't really know what it's like. I am sorry about the pain this may be causing you. But that doesn't deny the need for you to make this change . . . try this behavior . . . talk about this problem. . . ."

In short, we have no simple answer to the question of former victim vs. nonvictim leaders. There are pros and cons on both sides. However, our experience on a very practical level says that it is difficult to find enough group leaders of either kind to meet the demand. The question which must be asked of nonvictim leaders is whether they can be understanding and empathic enough to gain the confidence of the group members.

For former victim leaders the questions are whether they have resolved their own developmental issues resulting from their abuse and clarified their feelings about themselves and their parents. Are they able to achieve adequate distance from their own experience so that they do not confuse their own emotions and experiences with those of the members of the group? If they have accomplished this, then they clearly have the edge over a nonvictim leader in understanding and appreciating the ramifications of an abusive past.

FIRM

Thus far we have described group leaders as persons who must be understanding, empathic, and warm. These qualities are essential, but this does not mean leaders can be soft-touch push-overs. While being sympathetic and sensitive, they must also be clear about their objectives for the group and its members and firm enough to carry through on those goals.

One of the first issues about which they must be clear is the structure and direction of the group. As we have noted, former abuse victims are accustomed to functioning in chaos and are, therefore, more comfortable in such an environment. This means it may take a special effort on the part of the leaders to develop and maintain a structure for the group.

It is particularly important to begin with a tight structure which can be relaxed later. It is very difficult to impose a firm structure after a group has been functioning without one. This structure should include beginning and ending exercises, time allotments for such activities, and assigned time for each person to share his or her concerns. We have even gone so far as to give various members the responsibility for monitoring the time. The advantages of as well as the problems with this approach have already been discussed in Chapter Three.

Another area where gentle firmness is especially necessary is in the process of getting group members to change destructive behaviors and to grow. This requires an especially delicate sensitivity to the deeply ingrained fears which the members of the group have developed because of their abusive experience. Most of their previous experiences of criticism and correction have taken the form of nagging at best and physical abuse at worst. Any criticism is seen as a prelude to violence. Any critic is viewed as a potential abuser. Therefore, anything which bears a resemblance to previous experience is immediately tuned out and the source of the critique is categorized with their parents. A great deal of patient interpretation and gentle repetition is necessary to get beyond this blockage. Clear and forthright statements distinguishing what is said and done *now* from what was said and done previously must be made repeatedly.

It is important in this process to be constantly reassuring about one's affection for the group member even as one presses for change. It is often helpful to point out that the changes sought are something the leader *wants* for the good of the group member. Wanting does not necessarily mean getting. The leader must emphasize that even if the desired result is not achieved, the relationship and the affection for the group member will remain the same. During this process the leaders must be consistent in the desires and expectations they express, as well as the affection they offer; this is essential to maintain a trusting relationship.

Another distinction leaders must constantly reiterate is that between persons and their actions. Even though they may not approve of certain behaviors, that does not mean they dislike the person. This distinction was seldom if ever made by their parents and, therefore, for the former victim doing something wrong means one is evil and deserves abuse. Therefore, the process of correction must be handled gently and constructively.

Our efforts to work with Tony demonstrate the complexity of this process. Although he looked about sixteen, Tony was really in his midtwenties. He was working as a busboy at a restaurant while trying to finish his college studies. He was very quick to share, in a loud voice and often graphic detail, his experiences of physical and sexual abuse from a violent stepfather. But he met any attempts to discuss the emotional content of those experiences with bewilderment and quickly changed the topic to problems his friends, all several years younger, were having in their homes. Whenever discussion shifted from Tony and his friends, he promptly fell asleep.

In spite of gentle comments about the rudeness and inappropriateness of his behavior, this process continued for several weeks. The group leaders finally pointed out that the group was not geared to helping his friends who were not present and that discussion had to focus on the needs of the people in the group. Discussion of the problems of Tony's friends was officially outlawed in the group.

Without the topic of his friends' problems to fall back on, Tony began to participate less and less — and sleep more and more. Confrontations over his behavior became less gentle. These confrontations began to take up major portions of the group's time and the hostility of the other members toward Tony was growing.

The group leaders finally had a private conversation with Tony. Although he had little comprehension of why his behavior in the group was a problem, it was finally made a condition of his remaining in the group that between the weekly sessions he would have to meet with one of the group leaders to privately assess his participation and to identify specific behavior changes. In these sessions the leader talked with him about the level of his participation, his attention to other people's concerns, the appropriateness of his responses to their issues, and the specific ways he could change his behavior to participate more effectively in the group.

Although Tony never fully participated in the group during the several months that he was a member, he did cease to be a disruptive factor and did pay attention to, and learn to hear and understand, other people's statements of need.

In summary, even as the group leaders attempt to be firm in maintaining group structure and pressing members for growth and change, they must avoid any possible appearance of authoritarianism. They will frequently be subjected to this charge. Most adult abused children's early experience of authority was autocratic and even brutal. Many of their current experiences with authority figures are, correctly or incorrectly, perceived in the same light. Being firm without at some time appearing autocratic is a very delicate process and one in which no leader will succeed completely. Once again, true sensitivity to the even mistaken perceptions and fears of the group members and careful analysis and gentle interpretation of the processes at work must be combined with extreme patience to overcome this block and challenge to the relationship.

ROLE MODELS

In all of these efforts the group leaders are called upon to be role models for the grown-up abused child. Most abuse victims have not had effective models in their lives. Not only were the relationships between them and their parents not worthy of imitation; in most cases the relationships their parents had with one another and with other adults werenot particularly commendable either.

The group leaders are therefore called upon to provide role models in many areas. Not only must they be the models of understanding, patience, emotional sensitivity, and the fair and unbiased authority we have just discussed; they must also be models for many social roles.

They will often find themselves cast in the role of parent. They will in fact become surrogate parents at various times, being called upon to provide the care, support, and affirmation that the group members never received as children. At times it will seem as if they are being asked to compensate for years of lost affection and nurturing. Even as that necessary parenting process goes on the group members must be encouraged to find loving, supportive relationships with other members of the group and in their broader community.

In addition, because the co-leaders of the group are a woman and a man, they will be perceived as models of interpersonal, heterosexual relationships. The equality and respect they show one another may well be the first such relationship experienced by the group members. The degree to which they are able to share the leadership of the group and support and encourage one another will be an indication of the forms such relationships can take. The extent to which the group leaders can be comfortable with and relate well with one another will constantly communicate a variety of messages about male-female relationships. As the group leaders good naturedly chide each other and offer support as well as criticism to one another, the group members will discover that male-female work relationships can be satisfying and productive. As the leaders confirm and complement each other's skills and strengths, these products of family dysfunction will experience the benefits of cooperative activity. They will encounter in concrete form the reality of mutual respect and appropriate interdependence.

In short, all aspects of a group leader's life and personality will be called into play in working with a grown-up abused children's group. Such a task is not one that can be done half-heartedly and inattentively. The hypersensitivity and high expectations of former abuse victims do not allow for such an approach. But the rewards are great. Leaders develop a profound sense of awe as they experience in a concrete way the complex frailty of the human developmental process. They also experience a deep sense of satisfaction as frightened, insecure "children" become confident, assured adults.

They gain a new sense of hope in the healing power of the human spirit as they watch group members confront and conquer fears, accept new challenges, and take control over their previously shattered and scattered lives. They are confirmed in their belief that proper insight and guidance can overcome even the most devastating childhood.

BIBLIOGRAPHY

Diagnostic and Statistical Manual, Vol. III. Washington, D.C.: American Psychiatric Association, 1980.

Erikson, E.H. *Childhood and Society*, New York: W.W. Norton and Co., Inc., 1963.

Finkelhor, David. *Sexually Victimized Children*. New York: Free Press, 1979.

Gagnon, John, "Female Child Victims of Sex Offenses", *Social Problems* (13) 1965.

Helfer, R.E. *Childhood Comes First: A Crash Course in Childhood for Adults*. East Lansing, Michigan: Ray E. Helfer, 1978.

Herman, Judith L. *Father-Daughter Incest*. Cambridge, Massachusetts: Harvard University Press, 1981.

Justice, Blair and Rita. *The Abusing Family*. NY Human Sciences Press, 1976.

Leaman, Karen M. "Sexual Abuse: The Reactions of Child and Family", *Sexual Abuse of Children: Selected Readings*. Washington, D.C.: U.S. Department of Health and Human Services, 1980.

Lifton, Robert J. *The Broken Connection*. New York: Simon and Schuster, 1979.

Nielsen, Terryann. "Sexual Abuse of Boys: Current Perspectives", *Personnel and Guidance Journal* (62) November, 1963.

Wilson, John P. "Conflict, Stress and Growth" in Charles R. Figley, Ed. *Strangers at Home*. New York: Praeger Press, 1980.

Wilson, John P. Personal correspondence, 1983.